MW01105285

MURDER MUST MERCIFUL

Essays on the Ethical Conundrum
Occasioned by Sigi Ziering's
The Judgment of Herbert Bierhoff

Edited by
Michael Berenbaum

Studies in the Shoah
Volume XXVIII

University Press of America,® Inc.
Lanham · Boulder · New York · Toronto · Oxford

Copyright © 2005 by
Michael Berenbaum

University Press of America,® Inc.
4501 Forbes Boulevard
Suite 200
Lanham, Maryland 20706
UPA Acquisitions Department (301) 459-3366

PO Box 317
Oxford
OX2 9RU, UK

All rights reserved
Printed in the United States of America
British Library Cataloging in Publication Information Available

Library of Congress Control Number: 2005922542
ISBN 0-7618-3203-3 (paperback : alk. ppr.)
ISBN: 978-0-7618-3203-4

⊖™ The paper used in this publication meets the minimum
requirements of American National Standard for Information
Sciences—Permanence of Paper for Printed Library Materials,
ANSI Z39.48—1984

Studies in the Shoah

Editorial Board

Editor-in-Chief
Zev Garber
Los Angeles Valley College
Case Western Reserve University

Alan Berger	Florida Atlantic University
Rachel Brenner	University of Wisconsin, Madison
Yaffa Eliach	Brooklyn College, CUNY
Irving (Yitz) Greenberg	Jewish Life Network/Steinhardt Foundation
Steven Katz	Boston University
Steven L. Jacobs	University of Alabama
Richard Libowitz	St. Joseph's University
Franklin H. Littell	The Philadelphia Center on the Holocaust, Genocide and Human Rights
Hubert G. Locke	University of Washington
James F. Moore	Valparaiso University
John K. Roth	Claremont McKenna College
Richard L. Rubenstein	University of Bridgeport

Dedicated to the memory

of the Bierhoff family

and to the memory of Jutti Ziering

and her friends.

Born in Kassel, Germany on March 37, 1939.

Deported to Riga on December 9, 1941.

Last observed alive in the police prison

in Riga, Latvia, 1943

"Presumed to be dead."

TABLE OF CONTENTS

Introduction

Some five years ago, Dr. Sigi Ziering invited me to lunch at an elegant Beverly Hills hotel familiar to all who saw *A Pretty Woman*. I was relatively new to Los Angeles and to my position as president of the Survivors of the Shoah Visual History Foundation. I had known Sigi Ziering because of his generosity to the Holocaust Museum where he and his wife, Marilyn, were founders and because we prayed in a synagogue that bore their family name. I had also known of his story because I had worked with his brother, Herman, when he was disappointed in a job he commissioned a German historian to write a history of the Riga Ghetto. Herman and his younger brother, Sigi, were survivors of that ghetto along with their mother. They had been transported there in December 1941 from Kassel, where they had lived as part of the Nisko plan, the Nazi plan to make Germany *Jüdenrein* by transporting Jews to eastward. It was soon overtaken by the "Final Solution to the Jewish Problem," the systematic slaughter of Jews in Germany.

I had presumed that I was to solicit Sigi and Marilyn Ziering to become an integral part of the Shoah Foundation's cadre of supporters. Sigi Ziering had something rather different on his mind. He soon told me that he had written a play. I had been used to survivors writing memoirs. As a gifted scientist and successful businessman, I presumed that Sigi, who was nearing three score and ten, had also written his life story and I was prepared to read it with interest and to critique it and assist in its publication. But Sigi had written a play. We spoke little of that play that afternoon, but I offered to read it and to get back to him after I did.

I read it with interest, ever growing interest, and could not get the play out of my mind. It gnawed at me as it clearly had gnawed at Sigi for some time. I understood its many characters and their points of view; that was the easy part. It was difficult, most especially difficult because once again I was the father of young children to imagine Herbert Bierhoff's dilemma and to contemplate Herbert's decision to take the life of his daughter rather than permit her to be deported along with the other children from the Riga Ghetto, to certain death and the unspeakable anguish that would precede it. As a high-ranking Jewish police official, Bierhoff had advance knowledge of the deportation and a clear understanding of what would follow. The privileges of rank imposed the burden of such knowledge.

I spoke with Sigi at length about the play and his plans for the play. I could give him little help with the dramatic production; there was a stirring performance of the play as a staged reading at the University of Judaism starring Jon Voight some six months later. But I immediately thought of Simon Wiesenthal's *The Sunflower*, the book where the famed Nazi hunter told the story of a killer on his death bed who confessed and asked for forgiveness so that he could meet his end in peace. Wiesenthal had written to some of the important ethicists of his generation — decades later he posed the same question to a new generation — and published their diverging responses. I imagined that the same could be done for Herbert Bierhoff — and for Sigi Ziering.

Several months later, Sigi called to tell me that he had been diagnosed with brain cancer — inoperable and clearly fatal. He knew he was going to die. He knew he was going to lose the brilliance of his mind, which had taken him from a Nazi prison camp to academic achievement — he had earned a Ph.D. at Syracuse and to the apex of scientific and business accomplishments. He told me of his impending death as a matter-of-fact; without melancholy, without any request for pity. But the silence revealed that the responsibility for bringing this work to its conclusion would be mine, no longer his.

Judgment — we are asked to judge a victim; we are asked to judge a man's judgment, not in the abstract but in the concrete, a matter of life and death, an act of love, not hate.

Everywhere Sigi Ziering turned, he was haunted by the question. Each judgment called into question the judge and the jury — and even the ultimate Judge. Elie Wiesel once wrote: "When wrestling with the Holocaust, there are more questions than answers," and certainly Sigi Ziering posed some significant questions.

The *Judgment of Herbert Bierhoff* consists of the play. Sigi Ziering worked on it to the end of his life, as long as he could. Read it, wrestle with it.

It then consists of a series of responses from rabbis and ethicists, philosophers and historians, educators and teachers — survivors and non-survivors, Jews and Christians.

Appendixed is the interview with Sigi Ziering that was conducted by Rene Firestone on behalf of the Survivors of the Shoah Visual History Foundation, so that you can meet the playwright in his own words, depicting his own experience. And finally, we have included words of tribute from his daughter, one of his four children who spoke at the inauguration of the Institute that bears his name to explore the ethical and religious implications of the Holocaust. Alas, for while Sigi Ziering is no longer, his story must be told, his questions must be shared and his concerns must be enduring.

I suspect that you know that with this publication, the judgment is yours.

Michael Berenbaum
Los Angeles, California

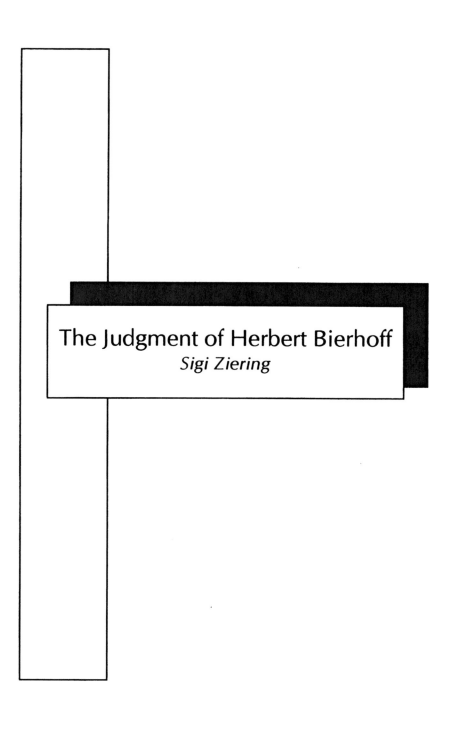

The Judgment of Herbert Bierhoff
Sigi Ziering

Preface

Memories of Herbert Bierhoff's decision to poison his child in the Riga Ghetto have stayed with me for these many years, usually buried in my subconscious, but surfacing from time to time, especially as I watched my children, and now my grandchildren, growing up. Eight years ago, during a vacation, I sat down to write a two-page outline of the Bierhoff case. With the outline in hand, I looked for a collaborator to work this up into a play, but without success. When I turned 70 years old, I decided that if I was ever to document the event, I would have to do so largely by myself.

Fortunately, I was able to interest Mr. Gil Kofman in acting as a sounding board, as well as in lending some professionalism to my efforts. The basic construct of the play was written in three weekends early in 1998. Mr. Kofman's patient efforts to critique each section, and the many valuable suggestions he offered almost on a daily basis, are deeply appreciated. Without his insights, guidance and constant encouragement, I would not have succeeded.

Scene 2 of the third act is a condensation of material previously used in an unpublished play, *If I Were God*, coauthored with Robert Baram twenty-five years ago.

Copyright ©1999 by Sigi Ziering. All rights reserved.

After reading the play Mr. David Dortort suggested some changes, which were incorporated into the present version. His many distinguished years of experience as playwright, director and producer provided valuable insights for which I'm very grateful.

As for the many friends and family members, especially my wife, Marilyn, who read this play and urged me to take it further, I want them to know that their encouragement not only prodded me on, but provided me with the self-confidence necessary for an untested and inexperienced novice in the art of play writing.

The valuable assistance of Mr. Paul Durham and his group in editing the many versions of the play is also acknowledged, with deep appreciation.

Sigi Ziering,
Los Angeles, September 20, 1999

Scenes

Act I

Scene 1. Sauna in a small provincial hotel in Germany, shortly after the Gulf War, 1991

Scene 2. City Hall in the town of Kassel, Germany, 1996

Scene 3. Remnants of the Jewish Ghetto in Riga, Latvia, 1943

Scene 4. The same evening, in the Bierhoff's home

Scene 5. Daybreak, in the Bierhoff's yard

Scene 6. Later that day, in the Blechplatz, the main assembly point in the Riga Ghetto

Scene 7. School building near Stutthof, East Prussia, serving as an emergency hospital, early in 1945

Act II

Scene 1. Shimon's home, Los Angeles, late 1990s

Scene 2. Shimon's home, Mutti's room

Act III

Characters

Shimon
A German, and six others at sauna
Ellen Bierhoff, age 5
Shimon at age 15
Herbert Bierhoff
Ruth, Herbert's wife
Kommandant Roschmann
Head of Jewish Ghetto Police
David, a survivor
Karla, David's wife
Miriam, Shimon's wife
Mutti, Shimon's mother
Kommandant Sauer
Oberleutenant Brenner
Prosecutor
Defense Attorney
Young German, from Prosecutor's team
Esther and Kurt, survivors
Mischa, Eric, Hans, Klaus and Yankel — teenage inmates

Prologue

This play raises many questions about human morality and God, with no apparent rational answers either offered by the author or expected of the reader. Perhaps the only response, if there be a response, can be found in the mystical traditions of the Hasidic movement.

There is a legend about the great founder of the movement, Rabbi Israel ben Eliezer (known as the Baal Shem Tov), and his followers. In a time of crisis, the Baal Shem went to a certain place in the woods marked by a stone, lit a fire, and meditated in prayer to ward off the evil facing his community. When a later generation was again faced with impending disaster, the Baal Shem's successor could no longer find the clearing in the woods marked by the stone, but was able, nonetheless, to avert the evil by lighting a fire and meditating in prayer. In successive generations, the Rabbis could no longer find the clearing, nor were they able to light a fire; but they succeeded nonetheless, through meditating in prayer. Many generations later, they could no longer identify the place, nor light the fire, nor remember the prayers but discovered that merely retelling the story was sufficient.

Our generation was not blessed with a *tzaddik* who could intervene for us to avert the Holocaust. Today, there are no markings, no gravestones in the woods, to identify the resting places of the victims. The religious fire has largely been extinguished, and the secret prayers have been forgotten. We are left with only the ability to tell the story for the benefit of future generations, and with the hope that, as in the legend, the retelling will prove sufficient.

Act I

Scene 1

A sauna in a small provincial hotel in Germany, a few weeks after the end of the Gulf War in 1991. There are seven people present as Shimon enters.

SHIMON

Guten Abend.

RESPONSE

Guten Abend.

GERMAN

(continuing the conversation with the others)
No, you've got it all wrong about this Iraqi thing. It was the Jews who managed to get us into yet another war. This war had nothing to do with Saddam occupying Kuwait. It was the result of a Zionist conspiracy to drive up the price of oil.

SHIMON

(interrupting)
The facts are that the Israelis did not participate, even though they were attacked; and that it was the United Nations supported by most of the Arab nations which made the decision to intervene, not the Americans by themselves.

GERMAN

Think of the hundreds of thousands of innocent women and children killed by the Americans. All Jewish propaganda just like Auschwitz! It was all arranged by the Jews.

SHIMON
What makes you such an expert on Auschwitz?

GERMAN
I made it my business to go to Auschwitz and find out for myself. There were no ovens. It has been proven beyond any doubt that millions could not have been killed there. All propaganda!

SHIMON
I am a Jew. I was not in Auschwitz, but I was born in Germany, and in 1941 I was deported by the Nazis to Riga, along with a thousand other Jews. Of the approximately 2,500 Jews alive in Kassel in 1941, only sixteen remained alive at the end of World War II. Was that also propaganda?

GERMAN
Then what are you doing here?
(laughs)
You don't look like a corpse to me.

SHIMON
(addressing the other silent Germans in the sauna,
and getting up to leave)
Nothing has changed. History in Germany is being rewritten again.

SHIMON
(addressing audience)
Finding a non-repentant Nazi in Germany did not depress me as much as the passive silence of the others in the group.

9

Scene 2

SHIMON
(addressing audience)

A few years later, when our company expanded in Germany and we dedicated a new building not far from Kassel, my home town, our German manager decided to invite the town's mayor to the dedication ceremony. He declined, politely, citing pressing business activities, but responded with a reciprocal invitation to the City Hall. Thus, during a trip to Germany in 1996, along with my wife and son, I visited Kassel, the town where I was born.

The mayor, some staff members and a representative of the Jewish community all joined us for coffee in the mayor's office. The reception was correct, but reserved. During the conversation, when we talked about the older part of the town in which I had been born, the mayor complained bitterly of its total destruction due, in his words, to "revenge bombing by the British." I had not come there to educate him on the history of World War II and the prior bombings of Warsaw, Rotterdam and Coventry, all of which preceded the bombing of Kassel. Rather, I was waiting and hoping for a word of regret, if not an apology, for what had happened to former citizens of Kassel. But none was offered. Yes, I was told, there were now approximately 700 members of the Jewish faith in Kassel, mostly refugees from Eastern Europe. No, I was told, there were, regrettably, no funds available to reconstruct the synagogue or build another one. Money was just too tight.

The last time I had been in Kassel was December 9, 1941, when a thousand of us were marched under police escort from the Schillerstrasse Gymnasium to the main railway station, for deportation to the East. Walking around the city on an afternoon 56 years later, there was little I recognized. My last residence there, an apartment building in the old city, had now become a modern

Bierstube. The former main landmark of Jewish life in Kassel, the main synagogue on the Untere Koenigstrasse, was occupied by a small, one-story block building and kindergarten belonging to the Jewish community. We looked for a memorial plaque, but could not find one. The former conservative synagogue and home of the Jewish school in the Grosse Rosenstrasse had vanished without a trace. Even the street had been demolished, and its former name had disappeared.

Of all the many memories of friends and family that I had carried with me for over 50 years, the fate of the Bierhoff family, fellow deportees, had caused me the most sleepless nights. On inquiring of the official records kept by the Jewish community in Kassel, I was given a slip of paper with the following brief facts.

Shimon removes a slip of paper from his pocket. Members of the Bierhoff family recite the following lines as they are successively illuminated by a spotlight and then fade into the dark again.

Bierhoff, Herbert
born June 19, 1903 in Burgentreisch
deported to Riga on December 9, 1941
presumed to be dead.

Bierhoff, Ruth
born July 12, 1915 in Essen
maiden name: Natan
deported to Riga on December 9, 1941
transferred to Stutthof in 1944
presumed to be dead.

Bierhoff, Ellen
born October 10, 1937 in Frankfurt
deported to Riga on December 9, 1941
presumed to be dead.

SHIMON
(addressing audience again)

So much for the official records. Let me now try to tell you the Bierhoff story as reconstructed from facts known to me and others who were there, as well as from recurring dreams and nightmares I have had in the past 50 years.

Scene 3

SHIMON
(addressing audience)
It is now the fall of 1943 in the remnants of the Jewish Ghetto in Riga, Latvia. The Germans are suffering severe defeats on the Eastern Front and, while in a so-called strategic withdrawal, are more intent than ever to complete the "Final Solution." Towards this end, the Ghetto is being dissolved, and its inhabitants are being transferred to Kaiserwald, a newly created concentration camp in Riga, as well as to various other destinations. Repeated "Actions" have reduced the Ghetto population to but a few hundred Jews, among them a small number of children who miraculously have survived the repeated "Selections," in which they and the elderly were the primary targets.

Ellen Bierhoff, 5 years old, is one of the few child survivors hiding in the Ghetto. She has survived mostly by luck, but also on account of her father's, Herbert Bierhoff's, privileged position as a member of the Jewish Ghetto police. She is hiding under a trap door.

Shimon, as a young boy of 15, enters a room in the Riga Ghetto. It is noon. He approaches Ellen's hiding place in the sparsely furnished room, knocking in a prearranged rhythm on the trap door. There is no response. Shimon knocks again. Still no response. And then again, more forcefully.

SHIMON
Ellen, Ellen. Please answer.
(finally there is a slight response)
Beautiful Ellen, come out. I have a surprise for you, and it's safe.

The trap door opens, and Ellen jumps into Shimon's arms.

ELLEN

What surprise? What is it?

SHIMON
(calming her down)
First tell me if you practiced your alphabet and counting.

ELLEN

No, I didn't. I fell asleep and had a dream.

SHIMON

Was it a nice dream?

ELLEN

A wonderful dream. Two white horses picked me up in a sleigh and brought me to the clouds. There was a big table with bread and potatoes. I could walk in the clouds, and all my friends were there. Misha and Jutti and Hannelore and Klaus. We could sing and play and eat as much as we wanted. Only Mutti and Papa were not there. Now, where is my present?

SHIMON
(hugs her)
First some practice. How many of you were in the clouds?

ELLEN
(counts on her fingers)
Misha one, Jutti two, Hannelore three, Klaus four.

SHIMON

And what about you?

ELLEN

Oh yes, that makes five.

SHIMON
(turning down one finger on Ellen's hand)
Now, if we take away Misha, how many are left?

ELLEN

Four.

SHIMON
(turning down another finger)
If we take away Jutti, how many are left?

ELLEN

Three.

SHIMON
(turning down two fingers)
If we take away Hannelore and Klaus, how many are left?

ELLEN

Just one. Now where is my present?

SHIMON
(turning down the last finger)
Now if we take away Ellen, how many are left?

ELLEN
(frustrated)
But if I am not there?

Shimon shakes himself, as if awakening from a bad dream, and hugs Ellen.

ELLEN
I don't understand. You promised me a present.

SHIMON
Just close your eyes. Here is your present.

Produces an orange from his pocket.

ELLEN
What is this? Is this a ball to play with?

SHIMON
An orange.

ELLEN
What is an "or-ange"? What do you do with it?

SHIMON
It's a piece of fruit, to be eaten.

ELLEN
(bites impulsively into the orange and makes a face)
It's bitter!

SHIMON
(takes the orange and peels it)
You silly bunny, you don't eat the skin.

He hands her slice after slice of the orange as he peels it.

ELLEN
(savoring every bite)
It's so good! How come I've never seen one before? Where
did you get it? What did you trade for it?

SHIMON
It came from the Spanish Hospital Kommando. My sister
who works there organized it.

ELLEN
"Or-gan-ized." What does that mean?

SHIMON
Like stealing, only God doesn't punish you for
organizing.

*There is a scratching noise. Shimon instinctively tries to push Ellen to
make her retreat behind the trap door.*

ELLEN
Don't worry, it's just my friend, the mouse. I call him
Kasper. I feed him a few crumbs every day. Please don't
hurt him. *(finishing the last bite)* Oh please, can your
sister organize another one for me tomorrow?

SHIMON
(teasingly)
I don't know, but if you give me your pretty pink dress
we can trade it for many oranges.

ELLEN
You will get many more oranges for the bigger dress
from Mutti. Take her dress.

SHIMON
You do know your math after all.

ELLEN
Can your sister take me with her? I would like to
organize my own oranges. I will bring you one too.

SHIMON
Soon, soon. We will see. We need to talk to your mother
first, tonight, when she comes home. I have to go now.
Remember to be quiet in your hiding place, until your
parents come home and signal you.

He waits until Ellen is safe in her hiding place, then leaves.

Scene 4

SHIMON
(addressing audience)
The same evening. Softly, in a corner of the room, Mrs. Ruth Bierhoff, Ellen's mother, sings Brahms's "Lullaby" to Ellen. ("Guten Abend, Geh zur Ruh/Schliess die mueden Aueglein zu . . .") She then leaves the room for the outhouse. Mr. Herbert Bierhoff approaches the bed with tears streaming down his face. Ellen seems to be asleep. Her father watches her for a while, then starts to walk away.

ELLEN
(half asleep)
Daddy, you did not kiss me goodnight. Why are you crying?

HERBERT
I have something in my eyes; it is nothing.

ELLEN
I cannot sleep tonight. Sing to me.

HERBERT
I cannot tonight, and Mommy already did.

ELLEN
(hugs him)
Daddy, I had a wonderful day. Shimon came and brought me an "or-ange." How come I never had one before?

They're from the Spanish hospital. Shimon said he could trade my dress for many oranges.

HERBERT

Tomorrow you are going on a trip where you'll have many oranges, and all the food you can eat.

ELLEN

Will I meet my friends there? Will you and Mutti come?

HERBERT
(sobbing)

Yes. You will meet all your friends, and Mutti and I will see you in a few days.

ELLEN

I also practiced some math with Shimon. What happens when you take one away from one? I do not understand math too well! Could horses jump to the clouds, could they? I had a nice dream today about horses and clouds and all my friends.

HERBERT
(sobbing more strongly)

Don't worry about the math. When you grow up, *(choking)* you will understand. God could make horses jump to the clouds if he wanted to.

ELLEN

Where am I going on this trip tomorrow?

HERBERT
To God. God loves you, and Mutti and I love you. Tell God we love you.

ELLEN
(half asleep)
You said you'll be coming too?

HERBERT
Very soon, my love, very soon. Here, take this pill to make you strong for the journey.

Ellen takes the pill and falls asleep. Herbert strokes her head, shaking uncontrollably.

RUTH
(returns to the room)
What happened? You'll wake her up.

HERBERT
She told me a dream she had about going to heaven. They are talking of another "selection" tomorrow, and of sending us all to Kaiserwald.

RUTH
About going to heaven? What does she know about heaven? What are you telling her?

HERBERT
Not heaven. I meant to say her dream was about playing in the clouds with her friends.

RUTH
You don't look too well today. Tell me what is going on.

HERBERT
Today we had to transfer some of the old and sick to the Ghetto hospital. You know what will happen to them tomorrow.

RUTH
Don't worry. God will forgive you.

HERBERT
(*very softly, almost to himself*)
God forgive me? Can I forgive God?

Scene 5

SHIMON
(*addressing audience*)
Herbert Bierhoff is discovered at daybreak in the yard, feverishly digging a hole in the ground with a spoon. Next to him is Ellen's body.

The scene shifts.

Scene 6

SHIMON
(addressing audience)
There is a contingent of German and Latvian SS troops
and trucks assembled on the Blechplatz, the main
assembly point in the Riga Ghetto. Kommandant
Roschmann, addressing the SS, is interrupted when the
head of the Jewish Ghetto police and some Jewish
policemen drag Herbert and Ruth Bierhoff — Herbert
with an arm band identifying him as a Ghetto policeman
— towards the *Kommandant*.

ROSCHMANN
Is that him?

HEAD OF JEWISH GHETTO POLICE
Yes, *Herr Kommandant*.

ROSCHMANN
(addressing Bierhoff, and working himself into a fury)
You Jewish pig, you child murderer. The *Fuehrer* is right:
You Jews are nothing but an inferior race without any
morals.

*He motions to some SS men, and Herbert is dragged away. We hear a
shot. Ruth falls to the ground, sobbing uncontrollably.*

ROSCHMANN
(ignoring her and addressing the SS)
It is absolutely essential that you make sure no children
are left behind in today's Action, in order to prevent further
killings of innocent children by these damned Jews.

(turning to Ruth)
And where were you, you Jewish sow? Allowing your
husband to poison your child!

RUTH
(lifting up her head, she whimpers)
Please shoot me too, please....

Scene 7

SHIMON
(addressing audience)
Early in 1945. A group of Jewish prisoners, myself among them, has been liberated by Russian troops while on a death march from the Stutthof concentration camp in East Prussia. While recuperating, I am told of a nearby school building where the Russians have set up an emergency hospital for Jewish women, also liberated from Stutthof. I go there to see if anyone I know has survived. To my surprise, I discover Ruth Bierhoff among the few survivors, but in critical condition due to typhus. When I approach her cot, I find her heavily sedated.

RUTH
(in feverish condition, opens her eyes after a few minutes, recognizes Shimon, but is too weak to lift herself up, and whispers)
Shimon, my God, it's you.

SHIMON
(in tears)
Ruth, Ruth.

RUTH
God has sent you to me.

SHIMON
God. After this, you still believe in God?

RUTH

Shh... Don't say that. I just had a dream.

SHIMON

The past years were not a dream.

RUTH

(halting, and in bursts)

I know, I just had a dream about a heavenly tribunal. Herbert was being judged because of what he did to Ellen. The patriarchs and matriarchs were trying to convince God that Herbert's soul should be allowed to reside in heaven. Abraham argued that he himself was just as guilty when he lifted the knife to sacrifice Isaac. But God remained silent throughout.

(pauses, and sobs as she continues.)

I was not able to speak. I tried, but nothing came out of my mouth.

(haltingly, after a pause)

Rachel cried throughout and finally said that the matter could only be judged on earth. Everyone agreed, yet God still remained silent. That is when I came back, and found that God had sent you to me.

SHIMON

God sent me ... to do what?

RUTH

I know I am going to die, and I really do not want to live any more without Ellen or Herbert.

SHIMON

Don't talk nonsense. You are going to live.

RUTH

There is nothing for me to live for. I only have a few hours left. Shimon, you must...
(lifting herself up to Shimon's face)
...make me a sacred promise.

SHIMON

You are going to live.

RUTH

You must find competent judges who will declare that Herbert was merciful and right in giving Ellen the pill.

SHIMON

What judges are you talking about? Where am I going to find them?

RUTH
(with obvious effort, whispers)
All possible judges, from the highest to the lowest on earth.

With a last gasp, Ruth collapses and dies.

SHIMON

Closes her eyes, and with tears recites the opening verse of the prayer for the dead. *Yisgadal, V'Yiskadash ....*
(after a pause, very quietly)
I make you a sacred promise to do what you asked me to do.

Act II

Late 1990s, in Lost Angeles. A section of the stage is illuminbated showing a gray-haired lady sitting in front of a TV screen. She is listening to a news report about a massacre in Kosovo. The lights in that section fade after a minute, and the main stage is illuminated.

Scene 1

Shimon and his wife, Miriam, have finished dinner at their home with David, a survivor, and his wife, Karla.

KARLA

Miriam, that was really a wonderful meal. You are a great cook.

MIRIAM

Thank you, Karla.

DAVID

Just imagine what we would have given 50 years ago for such a meal!

SHIMON

In answer to your question, David, probably my right arm. But then, even if you had this meal in the camps, you would have gulped it down like an animal.

DAVID

I still eat fast, and most often too much. Is it gluttony, or an acquired habit from the camp?

SHIMON

Who knows? I wonder whether anyone has ever studied the eating habits of survivors. I don't remember ever reading about this.

MIRIAM

What I want to know is. why do all our conversations revert back to your camp times? Is there nothing else of importance? When are you going to be normal and put this behind you? Fifty years is more than enough. It is just not healthy. When are you guys going to enjoy life? You know, Karla, last night after reading one of those Holocaust books, Shimon thrashed around in his sleep and kept me up all night.

KARLA

That happens to David also, quite frequently.

SHIMON
(bending over to Miriam and kissing her lightly on the cheek)
Sorry about last night, sweetheart!

MIRIAM

This week, good friends of ours lost their adult daughter. While participating in the daily services at their home, for the seven days of intense mourning that tradition requires, I was struck by the enormous outpouring of community support for the grieving family. To me, it seemed like a healing process for the bereaved family — a way of putting a gradual closure on their loss. The thought occurred to me that the two of you never had the benefit of such a closure, and are still subconsciously struggling with the enormous losses you experienced.

DAVID
Probably very true. When friends and relatives died almost on a daily basis, grieving was a luxury we could not afford. It would have seriously impaired our ability to survive.

SHIMON
Very early on, when it became clear what the Nazis intended, we simply had to adopt this dual personality, for fear of overloading our capacity for normal and accepted behavior. It was almost automatic, since facing death so frequently, on a daily basis, was simply too intense and overpowering.

DAVID
Shimon, I read the new book you gave me, Rosenbaum's *Explaining Hitler*. A very disturbing book!

SHIMON
Why did you find it disturbing?

DAVID
For one thing, the animosities among the various historians and theologians that come to the surface. Each one embraces a proprietary theory, to the exclusion of everything else.

SHIMON
That certainly comes across. But isn't it the nature of academics to cling to a pet theory and proclaim it as patented and irrevocable gospel?

DAVID

That might be, but you expect some tempered caution and humility when it comes to explaining the Holocaust.

SHIMON

Since we, who were there, are unable to explain it, how do you expect those who did not live through the Holocaust to be able to explain it?

KARLA

Let's face it. The historians claim that you were mere eyewitnesses and as such lack the broad perspective that only a historian can bring to the subject.

DAVID

Indeed — the perspective of the professional historian versus the mere eyewitness! Look, as teenagers, we rarely asked such questions during our camp experience. We reacted, both literally and figuratively, solely from gut feelings. Had we pondered then the question of why, most likely, like many of the older generation in the camp with an intellectual background, we would either have chosen suicide or sunk to the sorry state of *Muselman* — the walking ghosts of the camp — with no chance of surviving.

SHIMON

I understand. But why not ask this question now, retrospectively?

MIRIAM

And if you had the answer, what then? Would it change

anything? Would it change your life? Would it stop this singular obsession with the Holocaust?

DAVID

I really don't know, Miriam. To me, nothing has changed in my futile efforts to comprehend what happened then, and why. Attempts to explain the unexplainable, to acknowledge evil in its most elemental and naked form, make me fear for my sanity, as well as the sanity of humanity. If we, the survivors, dared not ask the question of why then, and are unable to do so now after half a century of living with it, how do you expect an outsider to be able to explain the Holocaust? To me, it's almost like asking the monkey in the early space capsule to explain why he in particular is there, and what the purpose of the flight is.

SHIMON

You mean, in the spirit of Lanzmann and his great epic film of the Shoah, that to look for a reason — to ask the question why — is an obscenity?

DAVID

Why would it be an obscenity?

SHIMON

If I understand Lanzmann correctly, he argues that if you found a reason, it would almost create a mitigating circumstance for the perpetrators. Or, put another way. if indeed Hitler had a Jewish grandfather, his perceived sense of shame at defiling his racial purity would explain and might, in a totally distorted sense, justify his hatred of the Jews. Thus, his total war on the Jews might become almost rational, even logical. Once you look for reasons, no matter how contorted and convoluted, you may then explain and even, in a certain sense, justify Hitler's consequent actions. Explaining leads to understanding, and understanding leads to mitigating circumstances within a certain mind-set. If we admit to such mitigating circumstances, we are likely to allow future holocausts. Thus, you might conclude that Hitler was not all evil. After all, he liked children and dogs. The Shoah, in its magnitude and extent, was so totally evil that looking for pathways that would create and explain a beast like Hitler is, in Lanzmann's view, nothing but an obscenity. In my view, the only "explanation" is Elie Wiesel's response — silence.

MIRIAM

You might ask why scholars do not reverse their quest by writing books that try to explain extraordinary goodness in certain human beings — Dr. Albert Schweitzer, for instance, or Mother Teresa.

A baby cries, and the two women leave the room to attend to Shimon's granddaughter.

SHIMON

You know, David, I am really glad they left the room. Unfortunately, our wives are absolutely right about our obsession with the Holocaust. As an example, let me tell you what happened recently when we went to a concert at the Hollywood Bowl. I looked around me and tried to estimate the number of people present. A weird question occurred to me: did the number in attendance that evening exceed the daily killing capacity at Auschwitz or Treblinka? On the way out, I noticed a sign indicating 13,268 as the attendance for that evening — and walked away with the morbid thought that this was well within the daily killing capacity of either camp.

DAVID

I, too, have been uncomfortable in crowds ever since my camp days and try to avoid them. It is not fair to Karla, nor is it fair to Miriam; but I just don't know what to do about this, or how to change.

SHIMON

Coming back to our discussion about evil. There might be a fascination with evil; or, perhaps, by nature or conditioning, we accept human kindness and good deeds as normal, but regard evil conduct as a strange and abnormal form of human behavior in need of explanation.

DAVID

When newspaper pictures of a year or so ago showed Pol Pot as a crippled old man prior to his death, it was impossible to imagine him as the originator of orders for killing almost two million of his own people.

SHIMON

Exactly. Hitler and Pol Pot were once babies, and the temptation to ascribe their inhumanity to any external reason whatsoever is based mainly on our inability to face and acknowledge the capacity for pure evil in our fellow human beings. The mere fact that you refer to Hitler and Pol Pot as human beings, thereby acknowledging their inclusion in humanity, leads you to this dilemma.

Miriam and Karla reenter the room.

DAVID

If you follow this distorted logic of looking for causative, triggering factors in certain individuals responsible for the Holocaust, it is indeed even more remarkable that indiscriminate revenge against the Germans did not surface after the war amongst us survivors. Given our experiences during the war, we survivors had infinitely more valid reasons, based on actual facts and not mere perceptions, as in Hitler's case. One would have expected at least some of us to act on the justified rage internalized during our camp days. Suppose that, after the war, the world, in revulsion, having learned what went on in the camps during the war, collected all known Nazis and SS with their families and put them into camps, with survivors in charge and given a completely free hand. What would you have done? How would you have acted?

SHIMON

A tempting thought, especially in light of what little justice was brought down on the perpetrators by German courts after the war. As for me, however, I think I would have declined that generous offer.

DAVID

What if you came face to face with an SS man who killed your relative? What would you have done then? Or take it one step further. what if Hitler or Himmler had been turned over to you for punishment after the war?

KARLA

If you ask me that question, I would have killed them immediately.

SHIMON

I would have killed each one of them without the slightest hesitation.

DAVID

But would you also have starved and tortured them, or persecuted their families?

SHIMON

Probably not.

MIRIAM

Has anybody looked to see how Mutti is? Why don't you check on her before she goes to sleep?

Scene 2

The scene shifts to a section of the stage, which is illuminated. We observe Shimon's mother, Mutti, facing a television screen. Shimon and David enter that section of the stage.

SHIMON

Hi, Mutti. Remember David? We just had dinner together.

MUTTI
(highly agitated)

Do you know what is happening? Don't go out tonight. They are all on the streets.

SHIMON

There is nobody on the streets.

MUTTI
(pointing to the TV screen)

There is a fire. They are burning houses. They are coming for us! Where is your brother? Where are the children?

SHIMON

Turning off the TV and kissing her on the forehead. Everybody is safely at home. Nobody is coming, Mutti. You have been drinking too much coffee. It's time to go to sleep.

MUTTI
(to David)

I made some good chicken soup. Do you want to eat some?

DAVID
Thank you, Mutti, but we had a wonderful meal.

The lights dim in that section and illuminate again the main section, as Shimon and David return.

SHIMON
So much anguish in her old age!

DAVID
How is she doing?

SHIMON
Not too well. She is 97 years old, and for the last ten years she has been reverting more and more to the events of World War II. She is still totally concerned with protecting our family, and this remains her sole reason for living. She watches TV most of the day and takes any bad news as a threat to our extended family's well being. She misinterprets the news and often sees imminent threats to us where none exist.

DAVID
Poor Mutti! Instead of enjoying her family after all the suffering she experienced, she is still reliving those events. I wonder whether that will be our fate as we get older.

SHIMON
I hope not, but I fear it will happen to us, too. It seems that these long-term memories are deeply imprinted on our genetic material. I just hope they are not passed on to the next generation.

DAVID

Let's get back to our obsession with the Shoah, and to Miriam's question. Why indeed is most of what we read about the Holocaust? Are we still looking for answers to why it happened and why we survived?

SHIMON

You are exaggerating. But I do read a lot about the Shoah, looking for answers. And no, I still don't know why it happened and why we survived. Perhaps it was chance, and the eternal optimism of teenagers.

DAVID

How about the chaos at the end of the war?

SHIMON

What do you mean?

DAVID

Lately I have wondered why, after Himmler decreed a halt to the killing in the last few months of the war, most of the local SS guards still would not stop the killings.

Scene 3

DAVID
(addressing audience)
At the end of April 1945, we were in the Kiel-Hasse concentration camp. The SS, knowing there were only days left, stepped up their brutality, if that was possible. They had the women in the camp tailor civilian clothes for them. One evening, they shot 40 Polish officers who had been in the camp. On the night of April 30, an SS officer came to our barracks and selected two of us to come with him to the morgue.

As David continues, the lights around him dim. A second section of the stage is illuminated, in which the actions in the morgue are illustrated while he recites the story.

In the morgue, the SS man instructed us to remove the civilian clothes of the victims lying on the floor. One of the unfortunate victims was still alive. The SS man took out his pistol and, with the words, "You stubborn pig," shot him.

The lights in the morgue section of the stage dim and David is illuminated again, continuing his story.

We then returned to the barracks, and the SS man instructed us to exchange our striped zebra clothes for civilian clothes. He also indicated that the Swedish Red Cross would pick us up the next morning. We hardly slept that night because we expected the worst.

As David speaks, the lights around him dim. A second section of the stage is illuminated, in which the following day's actions on the Appell grounds are illustrated, while he continues with the story.

The next morning, all Jews were asked to assemble in front of the *Kommandantur*. We noticed some white trucks with the Swedish Red Cross flag manned by smiling and friendly-looking civilians. The SS were frighteningly civil and even made a farewell speech, as if nothing had happened, as if we were leaving a vacation resort. We were very concerned that this was a trap, but somehow the friendly expressions and reassurances of the Swedish Red Cross personnel made us board the buses.

As David continues, the lights in the parallel section dim, and David is illuminated as he addresses the audience.

That is how we were liberated. We were told later that Count Bernadotte of Sweden had negotiated with Himmler. There was some monetary transaction involved: a few million dollars for the release of a few thousand Jews. As always, Himmler and his thugs were for sale.

SHIMON

In my case, there are at least two specific reasons, I think, for my survival. The first one is totally irrational, and I even hate to mention it for fear of being misunderstood. Yet, I have often thought about it. When I was in the Kaiserwald concentration camp, one morning when we had five minutes to wash ourselves, I noticed a little old man standing in a corner. I remember wondering why he was not wearing the mandatory striped zebra outfit; perhaps he was a recent arrival. He was oblivious to

anything going on and apparently deep in prayer. I was
carrying with me a small prayer book, which I had found
a few days before. Why, I don't know, but I went over
and gave it to the old man. He broke into tears and
blessed me.

DAVID

You are a mystic after all! Was he a rabbi?

SHIMON

I told you it was irrational, and I really did not want to
discuss it.

DAVID

Perhaps he was a messenger from God, an angel? This
really tells me a lot about you.

SHIMON

I don't know; I never saw him again. But I can
remember that one-minute encounter of 55 years ago
as clearly as if it happened yesterday. The other reason
for my survival is the heroic strength of my mother,
may God bless her, during that period. She was a
tremendous source of strength for us. After the first
Selection in the Ghetto, she immediately insisted that
my brother and I volunteer for work details to get us
out of the dangerous Ghetto environment, at least
during the day. More significantly, however, after the
dissolution of the Ghetto, she ended up in a sub-camp
of Kaiserwald, ABA 701 (an army clothing depot) in
Muehlgraben, which was run by the Army instead of
the SS and was therefore somewhat less severe. My
brother and I ended up in Kaiserwald.

As Shimon speaks, the lights around him dim and a section of the stage is illuminated. In the following, actions at the ABA are illustrated, while Shimon recites his story.

Once when the commanding Wehrmacht officer in charge of this army clothing depot visited the place where she worked, my mother threw herself to the ground and pleaded with him to get us transferred to his domain.

The lights in the second section dim and the main section is illuminated.

KARLA
Did it help? Did the officer respond to Mutti's plea?

Scene 4

A sparsely furnished barracks room, with cards strewn on the table, an empty bottle of vodka, and a full ash tray. Kommandant Sauer and Oberleutenant Brenner, their uniforms open at the neck, having a discussion.

BRENNER

You cleaned me out tonight, but good.

SAUER

What else are you going to do with your money in this God-forsaken place?

BRENNER

The Russkies have cut our railroad in Lithuania. We are switching our supply channels to freighters on the Baltic. We might be cut off in a few weeks. What then?

SAUER

The Fuehrer knows what he is doing. How can you even imagine that these Bolsheviks are capable of winning?

BRENNER

That single-plane attack on the harbor came awfully close to sinking our U-boat today. But shooting the Russian pilot in midair as he floated down in his parachute was not fair.

SAUER

(with a threatening tone)

Fair? How can you even apply the word to these subhumans. Anyhow, we did him a favor. What do you think would have happened to him if he had landed? You know, I could report you for this defeatist talk. This is a fight that we will win only if we support the Fuehrer totally and without mercy. There is no room for Jewish sentimentality here.

BRENNER

I guess you're right. What do you hear from the family?

SAUER

Our home in Bonn was bombed last month and totally destroyed. Luckily, everybody survived in the shelter. The family moved in with my in-laws in the country. Hans was accepted by the Waffen-SS. I am really proud of that boy.

BRENNER

Did you try on the riding boots yet? Do they fit?

SAUER

Like a glove. How much do I owe you?

BRENNER

Forget it; the invoices from France never arrived. When I get them, I'll let you know. By the way, there are two boys in Kaiserwald who were held back when the Ghetto was cleared out. They are good workers, and I could certainly use them. Could you send them over?

SAUER
(laughing derisively)
Two Jews for two boots! Sure, give me their names.

The lights dim and the main section is illuminated again.

KARLA

Fantastic! So your fate was decided by a card game!

SHIMON

Yes, "two Jews for two boots." I doubt whether we would be alive today but for that card game.

There is a noise, and a different side of the stage illuminates once again, as Shimon and Miriam rush into Mutti's bedroom, where she is watching TV.

MUTTI

Shimon, where is Jutti and her friend Ellen? I just saw them. They were crying and calling me.

SHIMON

You must have had a dream.

MUTTI
(pointing to the screen)
Look, there is Bierhoff. Tell me the truth. What is going on?

SHIMON
(turning off the TV screen)
Mutti that is not Bierhoff. He has been dead for over 50 years.

MIRIAM
(pouring a glass of water)
Here, Mutti, drink this. You need to go to sleep.
Everything is fine.

The lights fade again as Miriam and Shimon return to the main room.

Scene 5

KARLA
What happened?

SHIMON
Mutti had a bad dream about her niece and her friend who were killed in Riga. It is not the first time. As she grows older, I think she lives more and more in the past.

MIRIAM
Is that not true for the two of you as well? Sometimes I think that Shimon is lucky for burying himself in his work and not retiring. I shudder to think what he would be like with his memories if work did not exhaust him.

DAVID
Remember the sign at the gates of Auschwitz: *Arbeit Macht Frei*. That is the price you both pay for being married to "KZ-niks".

SHIMON
You know, a few years ago, a German business friend who retired at age 55 asked why I had no plans to retire. I told him, tongue in cheek, that in the camps, working meant you had at least a chance to live. There might be a lot of truth to this statement.

KARLA
Shimon, what about that recent movie *Life is Beautiful*? I liked it, but David was not so sure whether he liked it.

SHIMON

I, too, had mixed feelings. The introduction was pure slapstick comedy, and you wondered where the script was going or what it had to do with the Holocaust. When it became serious all of a sudden, turning by 180 degrees so to speak, I had a hard time adjusting to the new mood. The fairyland, make-believe attitude adopted by the father in the camp to shield his son apparently rests on historical facts and was a very worthwhile theme to explore. That part was very moving. As a parent now, one can well imagine the incredible anguish all parents felt during this hellish experience. As a matter of fact, the father portrayed in the movie saved his child while he lost his own life. With very, very few exceptions, most other parents could not save their children. Unfortunately, playing the clown was not an option for us. It would not have changed anything.

It is interesting, though, that I have never encountered any comedy or humor in the writings of survivors regarding their experiences. Their experiences were just so overwhelmingly on the dark side as to completely rule out comedy or humor. However, for second-generation material about the Holocaust, as is the case with this movie, the introduction of comic relief may help both the author and his audience to deal better with the subject. Hence, my mixed reaction to the movie.

DAVID

The title itself, *Life is Beautiful,* turns me off. There was nothing beautiful or exhilarating about life in the camps. On the contrary, this was the seminally most devastating, most depressing human experience imaginable. Could the title possibly refer to the father's efforts to protect and save his son?

MIRIAM

I still think it was a great movie. In my mind, the sudden transition from a carefree existence to camp conditions reinforced the message and made it so much more poignant. Not having lived through it, most people, myself included, have only a limited capacity to absorb the full and incomprehensible horror of the camps.

SHIMON

David, returning to the question of the death marches and the chaos at the end of the war, my take on the marches is that as long as the SS pretended to guard us, they did not have to go to the Eastern front.

DAVID

Sure. When the game was up, the sole interest of the SS was to avoid active service at the front. As you know Kurt, too, participated in a death march at the end of the war in southwestern Poland and the Czech Republic territory. After four weeks of senseless marches, only 80 survived out of the original 1,200. Yet the full strength of the SS guards remained until the very end, when they suddenly disappeared as the front came near. So much for their heroic devotion and loyalty to Hitler! They could easily have killed all 1,200 on the first day and joined in the defense of the Fatherland.

SHIMON

Speculation, perhaps, yet it makes sense! Towards the end of the war, Himmler wanted to put a stop to the killing to improve his chances with the West as a peacemaker and successor to Hitler, yet he was afraid of both Hitler and his own underlings. Then the true nature of the SS surfaced; they occupied themselves with senseless death marches and killings, yet kept enough of us alive to give them a reason for not defending the Reich.

DAVID

We know about the SS. What about the Germans as a nation? Did you read Goldhagen's book, *Hitler's Willing Executioners?* Take that police battalion from Hamburg — solid, middle-aged burghers, only a few of them Nazi party members, and many of them trained as policemen to uphold the law. Yet they willingly killed hundreds of thousands, including women and children. Only a handful refused, and nothing happened to them.

KARLA

Again a book about the Holocaust. There's no end to it. Sometimes I feel like hiding all these books from David. Lately, whenever I read the book review section of the weekend paper, invariably there is a new title on the Shoah. When will it end?

DAVID

I don't have an answer for you, Karla. Unlike the immediate postwar era, discussion of the Holocaust today no longer seems taboo. On the contrary, it appears that as we enter the twenty-first century, mankind is still trying to rationalize this most singular and frightening event of the twentieth century.

MIRIAM

I have given up reading these books. It is just like an unending Yom Kippur.

SHIMON

Yes, I read Goldhagen's book. They even took pictures; and some of these civilized burghers brought their wives along.

KARLA

Unbelievable! They actually brought their wives along to watch the killings?

SHIMON

Goldhagen's thesis does not surprise me. Of course the Germans knew. I read the recent autobiography by von Weizsaecker, the former president of Germany. In it he recalls that early in the war, in the fall of 1942, a fellow officer in his army group witnessed a mass shooting of civilians — Jews — in the occupied territory in Russia.

DAVID

Yet they continued fighting for the Fatherland. Apparently, as officers, the oath to Hitler superceded any human considerations. Isn't von Weizsaecker the one who apologized a few years ago?

SHIMON

Yes, that's him. Of course they knew. Remember that during the Ghetto time in Riga, we were working with German army and civilian personnel numbering in the thousands, and they all knew what was happening. Multiply this by the hundreds of ghettos and camps throughout Europe — and tell me they had no idea!

DAVID

I remember reading about Albert Speer, Hitler's

Minister of Armaments and War Production, who suffered from a convenient case of "amnesia" at the Nuremberg Trials. There he claimed to have been unaware of what went on in the camps until exposed to testimony during the trials. This defense saved his neck and got him off with just twenty years. Yet, in his memoirs, Speer admits to having visited both the Dora camp and Mauthausen. Just as revealing was his conduct during the last few months of the war, when he actively defied Hitler's scorched earth policy, but would not lift a finger to enforce even minimal living conditions for slave laborers and concentration camp inmates who were being worked to death in the defense industry reporting to him.

SHIMON

It makes for an interesting contrast that, in a small country like Denmark, with relatively minor atrocities compared to the rest of Europe, the whole Danish nation knew overnight when they were coming for the Jews. And, more importantly, the Danes reacted.

DAVID

Yet they had Danish SS volunteers. I was beaten up by one.

SHIMON

There is always a fringe element of fanatics in every nation. The point, however, is that as a nation, the Danes did not have those historically inbred feelings of hatred against their fellow citizens, the Jews. What happened in Germany could not have happened in Denmark, in Holland or in Bulgaria, to name just a few countries.

DAVID

How could these killers face themselves for the rest of
their lives? How could they face their children?

SHIMON

I really don't know. When an article about me appeared
in a newspaper in my hometown Kassel last year, the
reporter printed an interview the next day with a former
SS man a year older than me and from the same
neighborhood. He expressed an interest to meet with
me, but wanted to remain anonymous for fear of
retaliation by his neighbors.

DAVID

Did you agree to meet with him?

SHIMON

I didn't know what to do. After all, this would not have
been a social meeting over a glass of beer by opposing
football teams after a match. Finally, I decided to write
to him, to try and find out why he wanted to meet me.

DAVID

Did he answer?

SHIMON

After a long time, I got a response from him. It was a
rather strange communication. He seemed to regret what
had happened to the Jews. He also pleaded for the world
not to condemn the German nation for what occurred
during World War II. Most remarkably, however, he
claimed that he did not know until after the end of the
war what went on in the camps.

DAVID

Really! An SS man who did not know? Did you respond?

SHIMON

I replied that I could not understand his desire for anonymity, and absolutely could not believe he had no knowledge of the camps during the war. I haven't heard from him since.

DAVID

Coming back to the Germans and what they did or did not know, don't you have a letter written by the Daimler Benz service center in Riga during the war to the Ghetto Kommandantur requesting specific pieces of furniture from the Ghetto?

SHIMON

Exactly. And this was a civilian support agency, which not only knew what was going on, but shamelessly tried to profit from it. That is why I've never bought a Mercedes.

MIRIAM

What about the Swiss settlement and the recent offers of restitution by German corporations and banks which were implicated in slave labor and profits from the Holocaust?

SHIMON

Too late by about 50 years. Most of the potential beneficiaries are long dead.

DAVID

As long as the funds are properly used, to make the life

of needy survivors easier in the few years they have left, or for general educational purposes concerning the Holocaust, that is fine.

KARLA

Also disturbing is the eagerness of some in the legal profession to launch class action suits — some of them motivated by greed — and to fight amongst themselves for a share of the pie.

MIRIAM

I could not agree with you more. It leaves a bitter taste in my mouth since it gives the appearance to the outside world that the Holocaust is all about money. I would much rather have an apology from some of these institutions. No amount of money can ever undo what happened during the Shoah.

SHIMON

What disturbs me even more are the recent statements by some politicians in both Switzerland and Germany implying that this is "hush" money to prevent another Jewish economic conspiracy against their respective countries. Sounds like Hitler's propaganda all over!

DAVID

Yet, you are leaving again for Germany next week. How can you face them?

SHIMON

Very hard to answer. I decided early on that condemning all Germans would make me guilty of subscribing to Nazi-like racial teachings and prejudices. Yet I still feel uncomfortable with the older generation, asking myself where were they during the war? What were they doing? Discussion with the older generation is difficult, since invariably it turns to their sufferings during the war. the bombing of Dresden, for example, or the raping of their women by the Russians. Having been in the East during the war, we certainly know how brutally the Russians were treated by the Nazis: An estimated two to three million Russian prisoners of war were either killed or starved to death.

It is different with the younger generation; here there is hope. Yet they know so little of what happened. I feel sorry for them, since talking to them invariably means destroying their faith in their parents and grandparents. In a sense, they are very much like our own children, and have difficulties facing their parents' pasts just as our children have difficulties facing ours — though the reasons are very, very different.

A baby cries in the next rook. Miriam and Karla leave the room to attend the baby.

DAVID

You, of all people, feeling sorry for the Germans? Aren't you mixing up the perpetrators and the victims.

SHIMON

Just think about it. I was totally astounded at the demonstrations and civil disobedience back in the days of the Vietnam War in this country. Then, too, it was the younger generation, which questioned the war and caused it to stop. Watching the outcome, I gained respect for democracy. What Germany needs, in my opinion, is a couple of generations of a democratic environment.

DAVID

What if you had been born a non-Jew in Germany? How would you have acted?

SHIMON

You can play this "what if" game on your computer with business situations, but you cannot apply it to matters of life and death. In the end, we all have to take responsibility for our own actions. Otherwise everything disappears in a moral morass, and...

From the next room, we hear Miriam tying to rock their granddaughter to sleep, softly humming Brahms's "Lullaby." Shimon stops the conversation and becomes transfixed while listening to the lullaby. Tears come to his eyes. He motions David to be quiet.

SHIMON

Shh... Shh....

DAVID

What is it Shimon? Don't you feel well?

SHIMON
(wiping the tears from his eyes)
This melody, this lullaby, reminds me of something that happened in the Riga Ghetto, in 1943, to a friend of my cousin Jutti. It happened to a five-year-old girl named Ellen, who was poisoned by her father the night before the last Ghetto Action. I often dream of her, and of her father. If there is one incident that sticks in my mind and epitomizes what happened then, it is Ellen's fate.

SHIMON
(addressing audience, as lights dim for a moment)
I related to David the particulars of Ellen's death, as well
as her father's death, and the promise I made to Ruth in
1945 on her deathbed.

DAVID
It is an impossible promise that nobody can expect you
to fulfill. The father's soul looking for salvation? I did
not think that you, after all you went through, would
still believe in this supernatural gobbledygook. Are you
going to have a German court try the father's soul?

SHIMON
I already tried the Germans, but gave up.

DAVID
What happened?

Scene 6

SHIMON
(addressing audience)
The year is 1980 in Los Angeles. I have been asked by the German Consulate to meet with a group of German judges, prosecutors, defense attorneys and the German Consulate in the library of the Goethe Institute. They want to question me as a potential witness in the case of an SS man from the Stutthof camp accused of excessive brutality and wanton killing of inmates.

PROSECUTOR
You were in the children's barracks and observed the killing of the two boys for hiding some potatoes in their bunk?

SHIMON
No, I was in the barracks next door, and heard about it from the other children.

DEFENSE ATTORNEY
Then it cannot be admitted as evidence, since you were not present when the alleged killing of the *Häftlinge* took place.

SHIMON
First, if I had been in the children's barracks, I would not be alive today.
(getting highly agitated, and standing up as though to leave)
And how dare you call them *Häftlinge!* Call them "victims" or, more appropriately, "innocent victims," but don't ever defame those innocent little children by

referring to them as *Häftlinge*. For what crime were they there? Do you have children? Would you tolerate someone referring to your children as *Häftlinge?*

Shimon starts to leave the room; the senior judge calls for a recess. A young man from the Prosecutors team follows Shimon to the next room and offers him a cigarette.

YOUNG GERMAN
An unfortunate choice of words.

SHIMON
An unacceptable and, in this case, derogatory choice of words. Have you learned nothing? Is Hitler's propaganda still alive? How can you even consider calling these unfortunate and innocent children *Häftlinge*, with the implied presumption of guilt?

YOUNG GERMAN
I am deeply sorry. Just a very unfortunate choice of words which we use in investigations as a result of our training. There really was no presumption of guilt on our part. It is so hard to deal with this subject; there are no guidelines, no directives. There is not even a proper language for it.

SHIMON
(reflective and calmer)
You must understand, the psychological impact of endless morning and evening roll calls in rain or snow with the refrain "*Häftlinge*, Caps up! Caps down! Caps up! Caps down!" for hours without end. It conditioned us to believe that we were actually criminals. But to apply this term to children?

61

Shimon becomes much calmer, and the young German orders some coffee. Scene 4 of Act 1 repeats in parallel on stage, with dim lights and without narration, as the following scene unfolds.

SHIMON
(addressing audience)
I suddenly remembered the promise I had made to Ruth on her deathbed. The German seemed sympathetic, and I decided to consult with him about the possibility of finding a German court to judge Herbert's restless soul. I then proceeded to tell him the story of the circumstances surrounding Ellen's death and the promise I made to Ruth.

YOUNG GERMAN
(appears deeply moved and struggles for words. After a pause...)
Let me tell you something about the German court system. There is a case involving a Dutch citizen who joined the SS during World War II, became a camp guard, committed atrocities and murder, was convicted by a Dutch court to life imprisonment, and managed to escape from the Dutch prison to Germany. The Dutch have been trying to get him extradited for years and guess what?

SHIMON
Well, surely they must have sent him back to prison in Holland.

YOUNG GERMAN
There is a decree, a law passed by Hitler during World War II, that automatically made all foreign SS volunteers German nationals as of the day they joined the SS. This law is still valid today and is the reason

why Germany will not turn Herbertus Bikker over to the Dutch.

SHIMON
(shaking his head)
Unbelievable! Hitlerite laws still govern in Germany? Were they not overturned at Nuremberg? Did you not adopt a new constitution?

YOUNG GERMAN
(sadly)
We made some changes, but that particular law still stands.

SHIMON
And the neighbors of this SS man, Bikker, know that he is a convicted murderer, and tolerate him?

YOUNG GERMAN
Yes, unfortunately. He is raising tulips in the German village where he lives today as a free man.

SHIMON
Come to think of it, I have heard that Latvian members of the SS, heavily implicated in the killings in Latvia, draw pensions from Germany, while their victims never received a penny.

YOUNG GERMAN
That is the main reason why I would advise against bringing this case in front of a German court. In any event, they might be unwilling to offer judgment, or

even opinions, since the accused is long dead. There are additional complications as to whether under the Hitlerite laws prevailing then, Bierhoff, as a Jew, was a German citizen, or whether the laws of occupied Latvia would apply. Given our sorry history with actual cases of this nature, it is highly unlikely that a German court would ever consent to offer opinions on what they most probably would consider a "theological" matter, involving a hypothetical judgment in heaven.

A section of the stage is illuminated showing Mutti intently staring at the flickering TV screen.

Act III

Scene 1

Late 1990s, in a living room in Los Angeles. Shimon has prevailed on David and two other fiends, Esther and Kurt — all survivors — to meet with him.

SHIMON
(greeting friends)
Thanks for coming. Esther, how was your trip to Israel?

ESTHER
Wonderful. I took my oldest grandchild along; we had a great time. I even met a friend of yours, Klaus. If I remember correctly, he comes from Berlin and was in the Ghetto and some of the camps with you.

SHIMON
Klaus. I haven't heard from him in decades. How is he?

ESTHER
He is well — talks your ears off! He told me some fascinating stories about the two of you in the camp, including one where you traded a truck full of raw leather for a case of vodka and ten salamis.

SHIMON
I guess he hasn't changed after all. We called him, affectionately, the "Berliner Gross-Schnauze" — big mouth. He was always optimistic and by far the best Organizer in the camp. However, as always, he exaggerated. What actually happened was that the two of us were assigned to a truck loaded with raw hides driven

by a "Hiwi" — one of the Russians who had switched sides earlier in the war. The Germans did not fully trust them and used them mainly as support troops. Anyhow, this guy drove the truck to a Latvian factory and traded about half the load for two bottles of vodka for himself, as well as salamis for all of us.

ESTHER

He also asked me to find out whether you ever heard anything of Yankel.

SHIMON

Oh yes, Yankel; I remember him well. Unfortunately, I never found out what happened to him, or indeed whether he survived at all. He was totally and irrevocably destroyed at a selection in Muehlgraben; he never recovered from finding out that his mother ended up going to the left instead of to the right.

KURT

You mean he actually watched the selection process? Was that even possible?

SHIMON

Not quite. I will tell you what happened.

Scene 2

SHIMON
(addressing audience)
In 1944 we were housed in an old factory building at
the Muehlgraben camp which was controlled by the
Army. One morning, we were asked to assemble in the
yard and strip naked for a selection process. A group of
SS, under the command of an SS doctor named
Krebsbach, had us march single file in front of him and
selected the elderly and sick to board waiting trucks. All
males underwent the selection process first, and those
of us not being loaded onto the trucks were herded back
into a large hall in the factory. About half a dozen of us,
teenagers all, went up through some backstairs to the
large, second-floor room in which our bunks were
situated. The windows facing the yard were screened
with dark paper for complete blackout during air raids.

*A different section of the stage is illuminated with six young persons —
aged 14 to 17 — debating amongst them: Shimon, Klaus, Yankel, Misha,
Eric and Hans.*

KLAUS
I need to find out what is happening to the women. I
can move a corner of the paper.

YANKEL
Don't, please don't. They are naked. You are not supposed
to watch your mothers naked.

HANS
If we only did what we're supposed to do, we would
have been dead long ago.

ERIC
Go ahead and watch. I want to know, too.

SHIMON
Let just one of us watch. Go ahead, Hans, since you have no relatives there anyhow.

MISHA
Big deal. We've all seen naked women before.

YANKEL
It's just not right. God will punish us.

KLAUS
Can he punish us any more?

ERIC
(as he puts his arm protectively around Yankel and moves with him to a bunk)
We just have to find out.

Hans removes some of the window covering and stares into the yard.

Anything happening yet?

HANS
That swine is taking his time; he's lighting up a cigarette.

Yankel whispers on the bunk, still being comforted by Eric.

Now he is starting. Eric, your sister is safe.

After a few minutes, yelling.

Shimon, Mutti is safe too.

YANKEL
(whimpers)
Please God, please God...

HANS
(excitedly)
Klaus, your mother is OK.

YANKEL
(with a forced cry)
Don't tell me.

There is dead silence in the room until finally Hans covers the window again. After a few minutes, during which Yankel sobs, Shimon goes to a corner of a bunk and brings a salami out from the straw. He takes a knife and cuts segments for everyone, giving the first slice to Yankel, who bites into it with tears streaming down his face. Lights dim, and the main stage is illuminated again.

SHIMON
There is so much more to tell about Klaus and Yankel, and of course the others. But that is not why I brought you here today.

Scene 3

SHIMON
(addressing audience)

At age 70, I am still haunted by the promise I made to Ruth. Some time ago, I had a dream paralleling the dream Ruth had in 1945 just before she died. Only, in my dream, Satan was present, mocking God for failing in the creation of human beings, and asserting that the killing of Ellen by her father clearly demonstrated that humans are inherently evil. Shortly thereafter, I arranged to meet with some other survivors at my house, to tell them about Ellen and her father and the promise I made to Ruth in 1945, and to present them with the case of Herbert Bierhoff for judgment.

David, Esther and Kurt, after listening attentively to Shimon, offer the following comments in somewhat accented English.

KURT

For heaven's sake, Shimon, have you lost your marbles? I do not believe what is happening to you. Judgment of Bierhoff's soul? A discussion about heaven, God, and a lost soul. Are you out of your mind? Are you getting senile? If you still believe in God, why not consult some rabbis? They should have an answer for you.

SHIMON

I already did. They have no answers for me. One tried to draw a parallel between Abraham's willingness to sacrifice Isaac and the Bierhoff deed, without getting anywhere. He alluded to the role Satan played according to the Midrash. Did you know, legend has it that Satan impersonated Isaac and returned to Sarah, reporting to her what happened, at which point Sarah collapsed and died? Frankly, I did not know what to make of it.

The next rabbi raised the question whether Bierhoff's love for his child superceded his love for God and allowed him to neglect God's commandment not to kill, but did not come to any conclusion either. A third rabbi broke into tears and suggested that I contact fellow survivors, as only they would be in a position to judge Bierhoff. Thus, in the end, the rabbis could not help and also remained silent, as God did in Ruth's dream.

KURT
What really burns me up is the belief of some of our religious fundamentalists fanatics, if you want to call them that that the Shoah is God's retribution for the Jews' not obeying his laws.

DAVID
If it takes the killing of one and a half million children to drive that lesson home, I, for one, would rather not be part of God's chosen people.

SHIMON
Actually, I don't blame the rabbis, since the circumstances surrounding the case are so far beyond their comprehension and may well be beyond the imagination of anyone except possibly eyewitnesses, survivors. And that is why I called you together.

KURT
Shimon, you have just made a very interesting statement about religion that may have some significance. When

the rabbis in the Midrash introduce the devil in the story of Isaac's sacrifice, don't they simply throw up their hands at something so evil that it is outside their comprehension and totally inconsistent and unexplainable within the context of their religion and experience?

SHIMON

Yes, I have often wondered whether organized religion can only pertain to a normal world. In the hell that we experienced, normal religious rules simply did not apply. That is why the rabbis could be of no help. Unless you introduce Satan acting independent of God or human ground rules, the rabbis operate in a vacuum and have no rational or religious answer. In essence, they don't know how to deal with an all-pervasive evil society that stretches their faith far beyond the limits. Thus, wanting to believe regardless of the facts, they are forced to invent the devil; and this, of course, leads to many other inconsistencies.

KURT

You seem to be mixing up Satan and the devil. The devil is more of a Christian concept, as I understand the matter. In our religion, according to the Rabbis, Satan serves as a kind of prosecutor, God's Attorney General, so to speak. Another role for Satan, according to tradition, is that of God's tempter or tester — as in the Book of Job, for instance.

SHIMON

If you are right in this interpretation of Satan's role, that would make it even worse, since he is then nothing but an extension of God's will and power.

KURT
What you mean is, if you are looking for religion in an evil-incarnate society, you would have to build up a structure governed by the devil's rules of behavior.

SHIMON
Exactly. Or perhaps it is the absence of all rules governing humanity which fundamentally constitutes these Satanic rules.

KURT
But the Nazis had very precise rules. The irony, however, is that Himmler, in his Posen address to the SS elite in 1943, complimented them on their service to the Reich with respect to the killing of the Jews, and in the same breath, congratulated them for remaining *anständige* [decent] citizens.

ESTHER
Why even debate Himmler's perverted sense of morality? I want to get back to a statement Kurt made a while ago. What happened to us 50 years ago still haunts me. There is nothing irrational about Shimon's quest for judgment regarding Bierhoff's soul. Do I believe in a soul seeking peace? In heaven? In God? Probably not. Yet, not believing after the Shoah is as irrational as believing.

DAVID
I don't understand you, Esther. What is irrational about losing your faith in God after the Shoah?

ESTHER
A very personal matter almost as if I am afraid to live in

73

a world without God. The Shoah killed my faith in man, and perhaps also in God. Yet mankind, in my opinion, without some external moral guiding principles and controls, will revert to the animal state, no matter how highly civilized. While I would like to believe in the God who brought us out of Egypt and gave us the Torah at Sinai, I cannot believe the same God would have abandoned us during the Shoah.

KURT

You might consider different Gods, or a changing God, though neither is a popular concept. It is highly significant, however, that most of the perpetrators were good Christians, not some heathens lacking belief in God. Didn't someone make the statement that there is no God after Auschwitz?

ESTHER

Exactly, Kurt. But what frightens me even more than the realization that there might not be a God after Auschwitz is the fact of what a godless society is capable of, based on our camp experiences.

SHIMON

I dream about Ellen and her friends often. I have seen Ellen in my children, and now see her in the faces of my grandchildren. I see a little girl in the car in front of me on the freeway and remember Ellen. In my nightmares, I see myself as Herbert Bierhoff and wonder what I would have done in his place.

DAVID

I do not believe in God since the Shoah. And I do not

believe in heaven or hell. How then can I be qualified to help you judge Bierhoff?

SHIMON

Whether or not you believe in God is not relevant to why I asked you to be here. I have known you long enough to know about your love/hate relationship with God. Tell me, David, that you have no dreams about the Shoah, about your actions and those of others during those years. Tell me that your behavior on a daily basis is not affected by what happened then. All I am asking is, "How would you have acted in Bierhoff's place?"

ESTHER

Shimon already told us that in Ruth's — of blessed memory — dream, God was silent. We are not discussing theological questions concerning the existence of God. I have already indicated that I, too, do not know whether there is a God or not. But obviously, for the sake of Shimon, who has been troubled by this for over 50 years, we can voice an opinion, a judgment, just in case there is a God or whatever it may be that humans attribute to the God concept.

KURT

Esther is absolutely right. We are mixing up a theological discussion about the existence of God with our right to judge Bierhoff or perhaps, in a more limited way, to offer Shimon some opinions about a tragic incident that has bothered him for most of his life. Clearly, whether or not we believe in God has not stopped us from making moral judgments since the camps.

DAVID

It is clear that Bierhoff, as a result of his somewhat privileged position, knew beyond doubt the fate awaiting his beloved daughter in the next morning's Action. He therefore realized he would be unable to save her and chose the only way open to him, the mercy killing of his beloved daughter, in order to avoid an infinitely more brutal killing by the SS. If the same information was available to me, and under the same circumstances, I would have acted in the same way. It was an act of pure love, in my opinion. Yet I would never want to be tested in the manner that Bierhoff was challenged.

KURT

There are still the odds. The fact that I am alive today means that I defied the impossible odds against me. Otherwise, I too should have killed myself. And indeed, the question needs to be asked. Why did Bierhoff not kill himself after giving the pill to his daughter? Was he afraid of God?

ESTHER

Why single out Bierhoff? Why, indeed, did you not kill yourself?

KURT

Some did, Esther, as you well know. It was not for fear of God that I chose to stay alive. It was more — how shall I say it? — the habit of life itself, and the fact that, as a young kid, you simply did not ask these questions or have these thoughts. In that respect, the Nazis succeeded. You learned to live in that hellish environment and adapt to it as best you could. The will to live one more day or hour in this hell, to eat the next lousy meal, increased almost in direct proportion to the hardships encountered. Anything that would distract you from your total preoccupation with survival was instinctively rejected. There was, of course, a breaking point, the *Muselman* state of mind. But our youth was definitely an asset.

DAVID
I thought that we would leave God out of this discussion. God's complicity and inaction at best disqualify Him as an impartial judge, and at worst make Him an accomplice — if you choose to still believe in God. In the camps, either there was no God or He had given the devil a free hand. As to playing the odds, when did you ever hear of a five-year-old and her father surviving?

ESTHER
There were some children — for instance, some of the twins Mengele used for experiments — who survived Auschwitz. But then I must probably agree with you that it is very, very unlikely that their parents also survived.

DAVID
As a Ghetto policeman, Bierhoff undoubtedly had faced this problem many times before. Until the fall of 1943, he had succeeded in shielding Ellen from the repeated selections. What made him decide then, at that particular time, that it was hopeless?

KURT
Very simple, David. He knew that the Ghetto was being dissolved. There was no longer any place to hide. It was the end of the road.

ESTHER

Why did Bierhoff not kill himself? He clearly valued his life less than that of his beloved daughter and was willing to accept any and all personal consequences. We will never know how he felt about God, that is, whether he believed in God at all. One reason for not killing himself might be (if you assume he believed in God) that he deferred to God's teachings against taking life as far as his own life was concerned. However, when the time came to expose his daughter's fate to the brutal Nazis, he no longer could stand by and had to act on his own, independent of any commandments or belief in God.

DAVID

Maybe deep down he expected, even wanted, to be punished, and knew that the SS would be only too happy to comply with his wish for swift and severe punishment?

KURT

The argument is too deep for me, David. I rather think his whole objective at that time was to arrive at a humane solution which would spare his daughter pain and suffering. His decision to arrange for a merciful killing of his daughter totally absorbed his thinking and guided his actions. Having concluded that his only alternative was to put her to death in a humane way, this became priority number one, and left no room for either fear or concern for his own well being.

ESTHER

What about his wife? Why did he not kill her as well?

DAVID

Very, very convoluted thinking, Esther. As far as we

know, he did not even consult his wife before poisoning the child. At a time when a minor decision could cause instantaneous death any minute, we reacted mostly by instinct and not necessarily in a rational manner.

KURT

Let me play the devil's advocate and suggest one way in which Ellen could have been saved. Suppose that the attempt on Hitler's life had succeeded and that this had happened during that critical night when Ellen died. Let us further suppose that as a result, the German army had taken over and wrested control of all the camps and Ghettos from the SS in order to win favor with the Allies. We know for a fact that during the attempt on Hitler in 1944, units of the German army took control of the Gestapo headquarters in Paris, if only for a day.

SHIMON

Suppose, suppose! It did not happen that day, and Hitler survived to kill millions of additional Jews. Bierhoff must have known for certain of the bestial shooting in the Rumbuli forest of 29,000 Latvian Jews in 1941. He must have known about entire transports that went immediately to the forest, and about the daily killings in the Ghetto, since he had personally observed them. After all, he was a Ghetto policeman. Given that background, he did what I would expect any father would do: protect his child through mercy killing when faced with a certain and infinitely more brutal death.

ESTHER

Certain death? We will never know. The Talmud teaches us that saving a single human life is like saving the world. Do you think that applies also to saving a human life if only for a mere 24 hours?

KURT

Esther, you are bogged down in sophisticated technicalities. The circumstances prevailing then were totally outside anything ever encountered before in all the history of mankind. I did many things then of which I am ashamed to this very day, and would never do under normal circumstances. Yet I do not blame myself today. If you want to blame anyone, blame the Nazis or your God.

ESTHER

There is no parallel between then and now, outside of my dreams. After 50 years of so-called "normal" living, it is ironic that we, too, can only face the unimaginable reality of what happened then in our dream states.

SHIMON

You mean that, like sexual fantasies encountered only in dream states, the Shoah experience is, even for us survivors, so far outside the normal experience which we reacquired in the past fifty years that we can only face it in dreams? Ironic indeed!

ESTHER

Exactly. In my frequent dreams, I mix up what happened then by introducing my children and grandchildren into the Ghetto and camp experiences, participating in the deportations and the death marches. Yet nothing else is different; we all end up marching to the gas chambers or to the killing in the forest, anyhow most of the time. We are the living dead. To me, Bierhoff's action stands out if for no other reason than that Bierhoff acted, and acted properly, given the impossible dilemma facing him.

KURT

Yes — the living dead. A very proper metaphor for our post-Holocaust life.

SHIMON

You know, Esther, I also have similar nightmares. My dreams, much like yours, also invariably seem to lead to death. What bothers me most, when awakening, is that my behavior during these dreams, with few exceptions, is passive. Unlike Bierhoff, I do not act.

KURT

That is really my point. That is what I tried to tell Esther before. There is no parallel in human experience. You cannot jump from the abnormal state in which you lived then to the normal state in which you live now. There is no continuity, no transition; it is an Either/Or state of mind. In your dreams 50 years later, you are conditioned to return to the state of mind you experienced then.

DAVID

Just listen to Freud resurrected! I did not know that you were also a scholar of psychology.

SHIMON

Let's get back to Kurt's statement that there are no parallels in history. As a matter of fact, there are at least two parallels in Jewish history. Recall the 920 Zealots at Masada 2,000 years ago who chose death for themselves and their families, including their children, rather than submit to the Romans, under much less life-threatening circumstances. Most likely they would have been captured and reduced to slavery, but they would have lived. The second historical parallel occurred during the Crusades in Europe, when whole communities in Worms and other cities chose to commit suicide rather than face the slaughter. Yet we honor their memory to this very day.

ESTHER
It almost appears that killing your children for the sake of God is acceptable, as in the histories you cited. Are you implying that Bierhoff might have killed his daughter out of religious conviction?

DAVID
There are enormous differences. If you accept the Zealots' justifications for killing their children rather than have them face a non-Jewish future, or (if you want to believe) a future without God, how much sounder is Bierhoff's action when Ellen not only had no future at all, but also faced certain and brutal death.

SHIMON
Is there a message in our judgment of Bierhoff? Will this tragic occurrence give future generations a better understanding of what happened?

KURT
I am not so sure that the lesson of the Holocaust is forgotten. We have an international court in The Hague prosecuting Serbian war criminals. And we have recently had, in front of that court, a full confession from the ex-Premier of Rwanda regarding the leading role he played in the genocide in that country.

DAVID
Yet the United Nations did not stop the killing, in a timely manner, in either Serbia or Rwanda.

ESTHER
Do you think that Bierhoff will become a religious legend in the future, on a par with the Zealots?

DAVID
I have often wondered how the world, and in particular the Jewish world, will regard the survivors and their thoughts five hundred years from now. For the first few decades, we were conditioned to be quiet; or, more accurately, no one showed any interest in what we had to say. We were an embarrassment to the world and to ourselves. So we stopped talking about our experiences. We have even failed to communicate our experiences to our own children and grandchildren.

KURT
What were you going to tell them? That the world sucks? That with modern technology future Holocausts could be orders of magnitude more beastly, if that is even possible or imaginable?

ESTHER
We are all alive; we have all raised families, with children and grandchildren. Therefore we have made optimistic, pro-life decisions, in spite of our experiences, whether rational or not. I do believe that the world needs time to absorb the lesson of the Holocaust. I also believe that the magnitude of the Shoah is so enormous that it will

be impossible to single out individuals like Bierhoff there are just too many role models. Our function is simply to record and tell in a factual way, without embellishments, our personal experiences and the events which we witnessed.

SHIMON

After 50 years, you want to forget, yet are reminded almost daily by observing your own grandchild, or any child, of what you lost. Sometimes, I wish that it was over for all of us survivors, so that the world, too, might no longer be reminded of what happened so long ago. But we also know that our message is important, for the lesson of the Shoah has not yet sunk in. Has mankind really changed as a result of the Shoah?

Pause.

As for Mr. Bierhoff, no man was ever tested to do more out of love for his child. He did the right thing.

Another pause.

Or did he?

End of Play

Readings

Robert Baram & Sigi Ziering, *If I Were God*. Unpublished manuscript, 1974. Expands on the material in Act 3, Scene 2.

Roberto Benigni, *Life Is Beautiful*. A film, 1998.

Michael Berenbaum, *The World Must Know: The History of the Holocaust as Told in the United States Holocaust Memorial Museum*. Boston: Little, Brown & Co., 1993.

Folke Bernadotte, *The Curtain Falls: Last Days of the Third Reich*. London: Cassell, 1945.

Daniel Jonah Goldhagen, *Hitler's Willing Executioners: Ordinary Germans and the Holocaust*. New York: Alfred A. Knopf, 1996.

Max Kaufmann, *Churbn Lettland: Die Vernichtung der Juden Lettlands* [Latvian Holocaust. The Annihilation of Latvia's Jews]. Privately published, Munich: 1947.

Felix Kersten, *The Kersten Memoirs, 1940-45*. New York: Macmillan, 1957.

Claude Lanzmann, *Shoah: An Oral History of the Holocaust; The Complete Text of the Film*. New York: Pantheon Books, 1985.

Norbert Masur, *En jud Talar med Himmler* [A Jew Talks with Himmler]. Stockholm: Bonner, 1945.

Bernhard Press, *Judenmord in Lettland, 1941-1945* [The Murder of Jews in Latvia, 1941-1945]. Berlin: Metropol, 1988.

Gerald Reitlinger, *The SS: Alibi ·of a Nation, 1922- 1945*. New York: Viking Press, 1957.

Ron Rosenbaum, *Explaining Hitler: The Search for the Origins of His Evil*. New York: Random House, 1998.

Werner Schmitz and Albert Eikenaar, "Kein Vergeben Kein Vergessen" [No Forgiving No Forgetting]. *Stern* 50, no. 47 (Nov 13, 1997), 172-174, 176, 180. Regarding Herbertus Bikker.

Gershom Scholem, *Major Trends in Jewish Mysticism*. New York: Schocken Books, 1961. For a variant of the legend recounted in the Prologue.

Gitta Sereny, *Albert Speer; His Battle With Truth*. New York: Alfred A. Knopf, 1995.

Richard von Weizsaecker, *Vies Zeiten: Erinnerungen* [Four Times: Memoirs]. Berlin: Siedler, 1997.

Glossary

ABA: Acronym for Armee Bekleidungs Amt.

Action: A term frequently used by camp inmates to denote a "selection" process leading to death.

Haeftlinge: Prison inmates (German).

Hasidism: Popular revivalist movement which arose in Eastern Europe in the mid-18th century.

Hiwi: A term used for volunteers from German occupied territories serving in the German army (from "Hilfswillige").

KZ-nik: A term frequently used among survivors for veterans of concentration camps.

Mengele: Infamous SS doctor in Auschwitz, who performed medical experiments on twins.

Midrash: Rabbinic commentary on the Hebrew Bible.

Muselman: The walking dead of the camps—one who had succumbed to the physical and mental pressures and had spiritually given up.

Mutti: Diminutive for "mother"—widely used in Germany.

Organize: A term, frequently used in the camps, meaning to obtain food through illegal barter or stealing from supply depots.

Shoah: A word (of Hebrew origin) for the Holocaust.

Spanish Hospital Commando: Ghetto inmates working at a hospital in Riga set up by Spain in support of their "Blue" divisions fighting on the Eastern Front with the Nazis.

Tzaddik: Central figure, spiritual mentor and religious mediator within a Hasidic community.

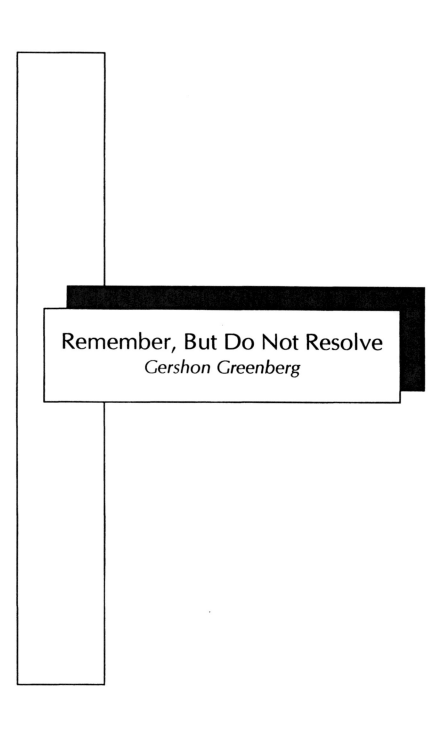

Remember, But Do Not Resolve
Gershon Greenberg

Remember, But Do Not Resolve

Let me share my understanding of the drama—and the valuable points I find in it.

Who Can Judge?

The motif of a trial provides the structure for placing the judgment of the Holocaust in the hands of the survivors.

Could the trial take place in heaven? With Jewish existence having become impossible in world history, was heaven the right place to adjudicate the catastrophe? The answer was no. Herbert's wife, Ruth, could utter no words at such a trial, while the matriarch Rachel could only cry.

Could there be an earthly trial? Ruth sought one, and urged Shimon to find competent judges—who would (of course) declare that Herbert was "merciful and right" in administering the poison pill. Shimon did not. The survivor David, in fact, considered Shimon's promise to Ruth to find the competent judges, impossible to fulfill. The idea of a trial in a German court was absurd—unless the trial would be used for the Germans to judge themselves in the process. The idea was considered by Shimon and the survivor David—but never pursued.

The subject itself did not belong in an earthly court. The Holocaust world was outside of history—and was not to be forced back into it. The catastrophe imprisoned Jews in the realm of no-choices, what Lawrence

Langer has called "choiceless choices." Herbert was forced to choose between seeing his daughter brutalized and killed or killing her himself; an "impossible dilemma." A German challenged Shimon: How could Jews have been killed at Auschwitz? What proof was there? And wasn't Shimon himself still alive? The dead were not there to testify, and the living bore counter-testimony. The truth, that is, was expelled from history. The catastrophe belonged to a "moral" realm, which defied normalcy. Stealing ("organizing") in the camps was not punishable by God—for it was not a crime. The teenagers in Muehlgraben (1944) considered the naked inmates in the selection-for-death process: The matter was no big deal ("We've all seen naked women before") or not right and punishable by God, or not punishable ("Can He punish us any more?"), and finally something, "We just have to find out." In this realm outside history, good, believing-in-God Christians became perpetrators—leading to the idea that there was no God after Auschwitz. In the Holocaust realm, SS guards continued to kill even after Himmler called a halt to it.

This was a realm of radical evil, beyond explanation. Satan could mock God for His failure in creating human beings, when it came to the Holocaust: "The killing of Ellen by her father clearly demonstrated that humans are inherently evil." In that world Satan acted independently of God or human ground rules. Normal comprehension shattered before such evil. To try to explain it would drive one insane. To try to force it into normal comprehension would falsify it. Or to impose reasons for it would reduce the crimes to functions of circumstances, which mitigated the crimes (thereby denying their pure evil)—when none existed. Indeed, such an attempt would falsely integrate the Holocaust into history and thereby establish the ongoing possibility of holocaust in the future (which mandated transforming the cognition of the catastrophe's uniqueness into the will to keep it unique and outside of history's normal path. The Holocaust returned the world to the point of chaos, to the origin of mankind's birth—such that its memories could be "deeply imprinted on our genetic material."

While antisemitism was enduring in history (the accusation that the Swiss money was "hush" money to prevent another Jewish conspiracy reflected a stream which existed before, through Hitler's propaganda, and after) the Holocaust broke away even from it. It was foolish to try to historicize it. When Shimon's wife, Miriam, spoke of "closure" to mourning, the modernistic term appeared out of place. The metaphor of a monkey in an early space capsule trying to explain why he was there, for the outsider trying to explain the Holocaust, was obviously out of place, if not offensive.

Could rabbis judge the matter of Ellen's murder? No, for their judgment would be caught up in a failed attempt to explain the tragedy—and they were brought to silence. When it came to the rabbis, "The circumstances surrounding the case are so far beyond their comprehension."

Could the judgment be left to God? No. When Ruth consoled Herbert and told him not to worry, as God would forgive him, Herbert responded that this was not a matter of God's forgiving him, but of his forgiving God. As a perpetrator, God could not serve as judge. To be sure, belief in God remained. Herbert asked about forgiving Him. On her deathbed (early 1945), Ruth told Shimon that God had sent him to her. The survivor Kurt rejected "fundamentalist fanatics" (an anachronism!) view that "the Shoah is God's retribution for the Jews' not obeying His laws"; and the survivor David averred that "If it takes the killing of one and a half million children to drive the lesson home, I, for one, would rather not be part of God's chosen people"—because both survivors believed in Him enough to criticize Him. The survivor Esther could not believe that the God who redeemed the children of Israel from Egypt and gave the Torah at Sinai could have abandoned them during the *Shoah*. Simon believed that his survival in Kaiserwald concentration camp might have been connected to his giving a prayer book he'd found to an old man, deep in prayer—who broke out in tears and blessed Shimon for doing so. But their belief in God did not express itself in terms of any divine role in history—to the contrary, God only remained silent. God, therefore, could not judge an act connected to history.

The judgment had to be left to the survivor. The survivor could not ask rational questions ("If we, the survivors, dared not ask the question of why then, and are unable to do so now, after half a century of living, how do you expect an outsider to be able to explain the Holocaust?"). But he held the one possibility for judgment. Perhaps the judgment consisted of silence—as for Elie Wiesel. While belief in God was thrust into limbo, the survivor was capable of moral judgment. As the survivor Kurt stated, "Clearly, whether or not we believe in God,

[this] has not stopped us from making moral judgments in the camp."
If it were up to Shimon to deal with Hitler or Himmler after the war,
he would not have starved or tortured them (the Nazi way) but acted in
justice to kill them immediately. The survivor Esther stated, that while
the *Shoah* killed her faith in man, she recognized (and still believed)
that without external morality, even the most civilized of mankind could
revert to the animal state.

The drama removes the possibility that Herbert Bierhoff could be
judged in heaven or earth, by rabbis or Germans. The existence of
heaven, as of God, is a questionable matter to begin with. There are no
words about the catastrophe which could be uttered in heaven (whether
because they have no place there or because heaven is not big enough
for them); and the catastrophe, an event of such radical evil as to have
no place in history, could not be presented for earthly deliberations.
The event belonged to the victims, to its survivors, who alone
understood—and who kept a sense of morality even when morality
was certainly abandoned by man, and possibly surrendered by God.

B. Herbert Bierhoff's Act

The author presents the evidence for trial—but any judgment is left
out of the drama, off the stage—for the survivor (who stands ever-apart
from history and even the history of literary expression after the Holocaust)
to make.

Herbert's act belonged to a point outside the division between life
and death (a division already obliterated by the living deaths of the
victims), on a bridge of love. He told Ellen she was going to a place where
all that was missing in this world would be given to her (oranges; all the
food she could have).

Herbert's act was a loving form of the *Akeidah* (binding of Isaac),
and as such far apart from the *Akeidah* of Isaac. In a heavenly tribunal,
Abraham would have said that, as he lifted the knife to Isaac, Herbert
poisoned his child. While Isaac was not Ellen (e.g., Isaac was perhaps in
his thirties; Ellen but five years old; Isaac had three days to inquire about
what was happening, and when he realized what was happening he may
have urged Abraham to go on; Isaac was not killed) and Abraham was
not Herbert (e.g., Abraham was commanded by God; he never had doubts;

Herbert wondered if he could forgive God; Abraham did not speak about the *Akeidah* after it happened), Abraham and Herbert were both ready to kill their children. But Herbert's act was of history, and Abraham's was primarily of metahistory. Herbert evaluated the facts (even if they were brought about by God—as indicated by his question about forgiving God), and concluded that they would not change; he was not open to a miracle. Abraham's trial began with the miraculous command of God and ended with the miraculous intervention of a heavenly voice. Nor did Herbert pray—to intimate a sense of the miraculous. Indeed, by acting decisively and irrevocably (i.e., bringing death) he assertively denied the realm of the metahistorical and the miraculous; and if God was responsible for the catastrophic facts, Herbert has no threshold for the possibility that He could change them. Abraham believed in God. Herbert's belief in God was moved to the outer periphery of his existential sphere. Thus, Kurt believed that Herbert did not kill himself because of "the habit of life itself," not because of fear of God—a habit, indeed, instilled by the Nazi ("You learned to live in this hellish environment...The will to live one more day or hour in this hell... increased in direct proportion to the hardships you encountered. Anything that would distract you from your total preoccupation with survival was instinctively rejected"). Esther believed that while Herbert's not taking his life may have been in deference to God's command not to murder, this command became irrelevant when it came to his daughter's suffering. Before it, Herbert was ready to act "on his own, independent of any commandments or belief in God." While Abraham acted unhesitatingly according to a heteronomous command to kill which defied his conscience as a father, Herbert split the heteronomous command to live (which he perhaps applied to himself) off from his autonomous conscience, which dictated compassion for his child. Herbert did not kill his child for the sake of God—as was so with the Masada zealots and Crusade victims, who killed themselves and each other out of fear of a future without political independence (Masada) or without God and Judaism—in the Abrahamic tradition (in the Crusades). He killed out of certainty about Ellen's imminent torture and death.

In essence, Herbert's *Akeidah* was an autonomous act of love, rooted in history. Perhaps he turned from God, perhaps not. But he surely asserted himself as the solely responsible, loving father, eclipsing God. The love also replaced the abstract right and wrong ("He did the right thing. Or did he?" The author states at the end—leaving morality a question, on the periphery of the drama), presumably introduced by God—and thereby removed God further. The survivor David put it this way: As a member of the Jewish police of Riga, Herbert could be certain that Ellen would be tortured and murdered in the next morning's action: "The only way open to him [was] the mercy killing of his beloved daughter, in order to avoid an infinitely more brutal killing by the SS...It was an act of pure love." Esther doubted the certainty—on traditional Jewish grounds ("Certain death? We will never know. The Talmud teaches us that saving a single human life is like saving the world. Do you think this applies to saving a human life if only for a mere 24 hours?"), but concluded that Herbert acted "properly." In any case, by his act, Herbert removed all doubt.

When Ellen asked where she was going, Herbert told her she was going to God who loved her, and that she should tell Him that her parents loved her. The drama concludes: "No man was ever tested to do more out of love for his child."

C. An Act Outside Judgment

Only the survivor could know the world of Herbert's act—and so the survivor alone could judge. The survivors were the living dead, they dreamed of marching into the death chambers, and so belonged to that realm touched by the pure evil of Nazism—a realm outside of history—but not of heaven either. The author does not let the survivors (Esther, Kurt, David and Shimon) pass judgment. Perhaps, because Herbert's act was contiguous with their own lives (of living death), making it impossible for them to objectify it. But the survivors could enunciate the substance of the act. It was one of courageous love, displacing the commanding God, and based upon the historical realities. Herbert wrested control of history from God and took control within the particular sphere of his family. This act of love removed the division in Ellen's mind between life and death—for in the world beyond into which she entered she would find all that she hoped for (but could not have) in this life. Herbert bridged between Ellen's present and future by loving her enough to kill her. Perhaps his act exhausted all the love he had—for he hadn't enough left even to murder himself.

Remember, But Do Not Resolve

The judgment of Herbert Bierhoff remains open. The facts are left with the audience to ponder—without "closure." Properly so, for the act of Herbert Bierhoff belonged to another universe. *It was left to remember, but not to resolve.* Shimon, unable to bring the matter to trial, was left to tell the story—again, and again.

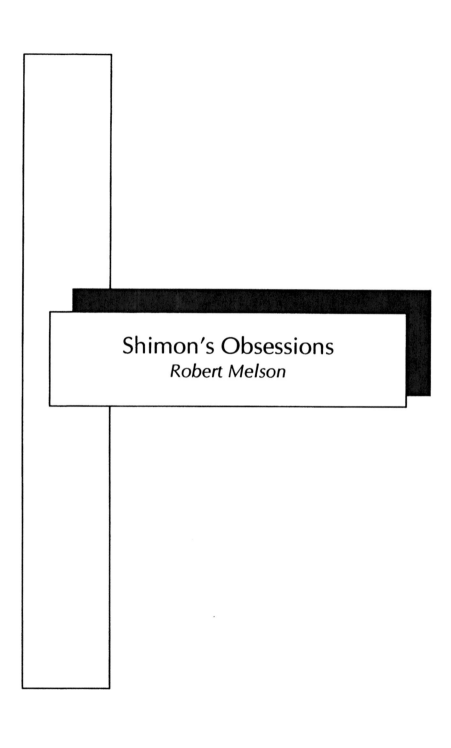

Shimon's Obsessions
Robert Melson

At first reading, this play appears to be about the judgment that should be rendered on Herbert Bierhoff who poisoned his daughter, Ellen, before the Nazis could kill the child, and who was himself later killed. Did Bierhoff commit murder or was his an act of mercy—a mercy killing? It seems to me that the question can be readily answered: Herbert Bierhoff may be blamed for having been a ghetto policeman, for trying to prolong his own and his family's life at the cost of cooperating with the Germans in the victimization of other Jews, but he cannot be blamed for the murder of his own child. Indeed, the more interesting problem is that of Shimon, the main protagonist, a teen-age survivor of the Shoah, who is saddled by Ruth Bierhoff—Herbert's dying wife—with the task of rendering a judgment on Bierhoff. Why does Shimon accept her request to stage a trial for her husband, and why does he obsess about Bierhoff's guilt or innocence for many years after his own liberation and survival?

Bierhoff's mercy killing of his daughter was exceptional but not unknown during the Holocaust. Consider Adina Blady Szwaiger, a young Jewish woman, a doctor in the Warsaw ghetto who worked in the Jewish Children's Hospital.[1] From the start of the Nazi persecutions she and the staff tried to keep their charges alive, but when it became clear that the ill and dying children were going to be rounded up and

---

[1] *I Remember Nothing More* (New York: Simon and Schuster, 1990).

deported with the rest of the Jews to Treblinka, Dr. Szwaiger injected them with mortal doses of morphine before trying to commit suicide herself. She survived—members of her staff found her and revived her—but reading her story one feels the terror of the choice that lay before her, and one is in awe at her courage and righteousness. And yet the children she poisoned, thereby saving them from a fate much worse than death, were not her own.

Ellen was Bierhoff's only beloved child. Imagine the depth of despair and anguish that he must have felt when he killed her to spare her the terror and suffering of a Nazi *Aktion*. Is this man guilty of murder? The answer is self-evident. It is articulated by David, one of Shimon's survivor friends, who says:

> It is clear that Bierhoff, as a result of his somewhat privileged position, knew beyond doubt the fate awaiting his beloved daughter in the morning's Action. He therefore realized he would be unable to save her and chose the only way open to him, the mercy killing of his beloved daughter, in order to avoid an infinitely more brutal killing by the SS...It was an act of pure love, in my opinion (Act III, scene 3, p. 76).

Indeed, the verdict is obvious, and one gets a bit impatient with Shimon's dwelling on it. Why can't Shimon perceive what David and others see from the start? The answer derives from the circumstances under which he was asked to pass judgment on Bierhoff.

We know very little about Ruth Bierhoff except that she was Herbert's wife and Ellen's mother and that she nearly survived. Shimon is briefly reunited with her after the liberation, when she is dying of typhus. In the hospital Ruth makes a last request of Shimon: "You must find competent judges who will declare that Herbert was merciful and right in giving Ellen the pill" (Act I, Scene 7, p. 27). The implicit question the trial would consider was: Did Bierhoff murder Ellen or was he justified in performing a mercy killing?

Had Ruth no doubts about Herbert, she would not have asked Shimon to arrange for a trial of her husband. Indeed, despite her asking Shimon to find judges who will find Bierhoff innocent—a strange demand to make of judges—her very request suggests that she may have blamed Herbert for Ellen's death. After all, Ruth nearly survived, and, given the chance, perhaps Ellen might have survived with her. Yet Ruth was not able to make the judgment on her own. Instead she gave the task to Shimon, a boy of 15, who had survived the lagers and was about to reclaim his life. She set him an impossible task—one he should have rejected from the start, but instead he replied: "I make you a sacred promise to do what you asked me to do" (p. 27).

On the one hand, if Shimon finds (or if the judges that he selects find) that Herbert was innocent and that his poisoning Ellen was a mercy killing, he may implicitly be accusing Ruth of having blamed her husband for the murder of their child. On the other hand, if Shimon finds that Herbert was guilty of murder he runs the risk of committing a grave injustice against an anguished father who was trying to spare his daughter from terrible suffering. Shimon's choice is to be either cruel to Ruth or unjust to Herbert. The choice is made even more excruciating because Ruth, Herbert, and Ellen, all are dead, murdered victims of the Nazis, while Shimon survived the war with his mother (we are not told what happened to his father) and is free after liberation to rebuild his life.

Only in the final scene, which takes place many years after Ruth's death and his burdening himself with the Bierhoff case, does Shimon himself arrive at the verdict that should have been rendered long ago: "As for Mr. Bierhoff, no man was ever tested to do more out of love for his child. He did the right thing" (Act III, Scene 3, p. 84). With that Shimon frees himself of Ruth and is presumably able to get on with his life, but his obsession with Bierhoff had managed to double-bind him and to sap his life of joy and vitality.

Imagine that instead of weighing him with an impossible task, the dying Ruth had said to Shimon the following:

> Shimon, my boy, I may be dying, but I am so glad to see
> that you are alive, that you made it out of this inferno.
> I recall that Ellen loved you so, and you loved her too,
> and because of that you are precious to me. Go try to
> find happiness. You're still a boy. A teenager. Do the
> things that boys your age would do. When you're a bit

older, raise a family. Have children. Teach them to be good Jews and good people. Don't forget us. Say the *Kaddish* for us, but don't become paralyzed by the memory of our death. We didn't suffer and die to poison your future, but to teach you that life is fragile and precious and that you have a right to your share of joy.

Had Ruth said that, she would have gone a long way to ease Shimon's way in life after the war, but it was not to be, and worst of all Shimon most likely would not have listened to her.

Like so many survivors, Shimon is left trying to unlock the secrets of the Holocaust and justify his life, neither of which he can do because deep down survivors believe that only the dead know the secrets of the Shoah, and only they can forgive them for being alive.

There is a theological issue that keeps recurring throughout the play: God's role in the Holocaust, and the power or rather the powerlessness of Jewish law to deal with an issue like the Bierhoff case etc. These are issues that leave me cold, not because I have an answer to the question of God's role in the Holocaust, but because I don't, and no one else does either. A loving, caring God was simply absent during the Holocaust and He may be absent period. I found it irritating and misleading and pretentious.

The just and loving God of Sinai was simply missing during the Holocaust and maybe He was always missing. Perhaps He was a figment of our imagination and we need to move beyond Him and accept that either we are alone or we don't understand enough about our own existence to know why He was absent. My own solution, perhaps because I am not brave enough to say that we are alone in a godless universe, is to hope that I don't understand and leave it at that. That explains why I find it irritating when people drag God into the Holocaust.

Despair, Murder, Death, Guilt and Anger
Efraim Zuroff

Despair, Murder, Death, Guilt and Anger

In most of the literature dealing with the Holocaust, the lines are clearly drawn between the perpetrators and the victims. There is no moral ambiguity involved. The Nazi perpetrators are clearly evil and guilty of heinous crimes, while the Jewish victims are blameless and innocent of any wrongdoing. The picture in this regard is quite clear and easily lends itself to moral and judicial judgments and the attribution of guilt.

This is not the case, however, in *The Judgment of Herbert Bierhoff* by Sigi Ziering. Ziering presents us with a story that either actually took place during the Holocaust or is at least based on the historical circumstances of the Holocaust, in which the traditional role of the perpetrator has been transformed. Instead of the evil Nazi who invariably commits the murder, the killer in this case is a loving father who murders his five-year-old daughter on the night before the Germans and their Latvian collaborators are to carry out the final liquidation of the children in the Riga Ghetto.

Can such a father be considered culpable? That is the question posed by Ziering who uses the incident to raise other questions that relate more to theology than to legal issues. As someone who has devoted many years to the efforts to bring the perpetrators of the Holocaust to the bar of justice, I felt extremely uncomfortable with the step taken by the father. Although he was undoubtedly motivated by his love for his daughter and his desire to spare her pain and suffering, in practice he took over for the killers and carried out the terrible act of murder in their stead. And though he certainly did not consider his act in those terms, we are left with the fact that it was he, rather than his Nazi tormentors, who committed the murder.

While I am certain that a fairly cogent case could be made to prove that ultimately it was the German and Latvian Nazis who drove Herbert Bierhoff to poison Ellen, the question remains why he chose to perform the act of murder? Was there absolutely no hope of survival in this case? Was there no chance that the liquidation planned for the next day might be postponed and that in the interim an avenue of escape might present itself? Although it was obviously foolish to be overly optimistic in the Riga Ghetto in 1943, was there absolutely no hope left for the Jews living there?

These are extremely difficult questions to answer and, in fact, it is practically impossible to provide an authoritative response. Thousands of survivors will attest that their survival during the *Shoah* was nothing short of a miracle, but who can guarantee that such a miracle was destined to save Ellen Bierhoff's life as well. After all, the horrible tragedy of the Holocaust was that we ultimately were short approximately six million miracles. Yet, nonetheless, even if a terrible fate awaited this five year old, would it not have been better to have such a terrible crime committed by the Nazis, rather than by a loving parent?

In that regard, Ellen's story is to some extent reminiscent of the debate over the activities of the *Jüdenrat* [Jewish councils] in German-occupied Europe. Should Jews have served on the councils which were created by the Nazis to facilitate the implementation of the Final Solution? Did the fact that the councils were able on occasion to alleviate the suffering of their communities justify their indirect, let alone direct, acquiescence in Nazi directives directed against the Jews they hoped to protect? These questions have been debated for years, both during and after the *Shoah*. The truth is that the history of each European Jewish community under German occupation was unique and that there are no ironclad answers to these questions. While some *Jüdenrat* leaders, such as Dr. Elchanan Elkes of Kaunas (Kovno), Lithuania emerged as heroes, others like Moshe Merin of Bendzin/Sosnowiec, Poland were considered tragic figures who failed to adequately respond to the challenges of the historical circumstances. But success or failure aside, the concept which ultimately guided the Judenrate and their leaders was their desire to try and save as many Jews as possible from death, which was not the case as far as Herbert Bierhoff was concerned. He had given up on saving Ellen's life and it was therefore, "only" pain and cruelty that he sought to spare her.

The key question is, therefore, whether Herbert Bierhoff's response was appropriate or whether he should have opted for the *Kiddush ha-chayim* (sanctification of life) approach advocated by Rabbi Yitzchak Nissenbaum in the Warsaw Ghetto. It was Rabbi Nissenbaum, a well-known Polish religious Zionist thinker, who when questioned whether Jews should follow the medieval model of *Kiddush ha-Shem* (sanctification of God's name) by committing suicide rather than be killed a cruel death by the Nazis, responded that under German occupation, the most important mitzvah was to do everything possible to sanctify life by physically surviving, since it was the Jews' lives that the Nazis sought to destroy, rather than their religious faith, as was the case during the Crusades. And therefore the supreme Jewish obligation during the *Shoah* was physical survival, the path not chosen by Herbert Bierhoff.

Perhaps it is not surprising that the protagonist of Sigi Ziering's play does not follow the path advocated by Rabbi Nissenbaum. If anything, much of the anger in the play is directed against God, rather than against the Nazi perpetrators, whose presence in the narrative is extremely minimal. "Where was God?" is the dominant theme in *The Judgment of Herbert Bierhoff* even though men committed all the crimes in question. Who, in this regard, bears the ultimate responsibility for these atrocities? Those who physically committed them or the Divine Being who chose to, or failed to, prevent them from taking place?

Having spent more than twenty years trying to make Nazi war criminals pay for their crimes, I believe that it is extremely problematic to blame God for crimes which were carried out by human beings. To do so, in fact, absolves the human perpetrators of their guilt and turns them, even worse, into messengers of the Almighty, a total distortion of the historical reality. What could possibly be gained from such an interpretation of the events of the *Shoah*? Is Ziering so angry at God that he is willing to deflect the major thrust of guilt from the perpetrators themselves to the Almighty? That would, in my opinion, hardly be an appropriate response to the crimes of the *Shoah*, because more than anything else, they demonstrate the absolute necessity for confronting human evil as forcefully as possible. By murdering Ellen, Herbert Bierhoff doesn't make God any guiltier. Although he does, thereby, reinforce the horrors of the crimes committed by the Nazis, at the same time he unintentionally (and unfortunately) helps them achieve their goals, thereby bearing a measure of guilt himself. By focusing his anger on the failures of God rather than on those of man, Sigi Ziering seems to be attempting to deflect the onus of guilt from where it belongs to a place where it will have no redemptive value.

A Haunting Question:
An Elusive Answer
Michael Berenbaum

Sigi Ziering's play, *The Judgment of Herbert Bierhoff*, makes us uncomfortable. It insists on something that we cannot deliver, that we dare not deliver—judgment. The Talmud admonishes, "Don't judge your friend until you have stood in his place," and we who are not survivors have not stood in their place.

No matter how much we study the Holocaust, something remains elusive. Modesty requires restraint. We have seen too many who have rushed to judgment, confident in their wisdom and their abilities, only to find such a judgment trite, shallow or contrived. The circumstances Herbert Bierhoff faced should fill us with fear and trembling. His decision was so personal, so painful, that while we can perceive his anguish, we cannot draw too close to the flames.

Rabbis have failed Ziering, scholars have failed, survivors have failed, and in the end, he, too, has failed. The playwright leaves us with the question and certainly not with the answer. It is a truism that the Holocaust imposes difficult questions and resists easy answers. Questions can be pursued together.

The fate of Ellen Bierhoff haunts us. It offers no closure. For unlike theatrical tragedy where there is a relationship between deed and fate, and a balance between what happened and what we can learn from what happened, the events surrounding Ellen's death—as indeed the Holocaust itself—are an atrocity. What we learn cannot approach the price that has been paid for our knowledge. There is no relationship between deed and fate, not for her, not for the more than one million Jewish children who were murdered, and not for her father.

Still Ruth Bierhoff, the bereaved mother and the grieving wife, insisted on judgment, and imposed that responsibility on a young Shimon, perhaps intuiting that such a judgment would take time and require distance. It could only be undertaken once healing had taken root and once the return to normalcy had been achieved. Ziering seems to intimate what many survivors understand that the return to normalcy is only part of the story. The "normal" self has taken its place alongside the survivor's self. As one survivor put it so eloquently and so brutally, "the self that entered Auschwitz never left. I left part of myself there." Any judgment would require a dialogue—perhaps more properly a struggle—between conventional norms of our world and life inside the Riga Ghetto on the eve of deportation, coupled with a clear understanding of what happened to young girls during deportation. The playwright, Sigi Ziering of blessed memory, waited until near the end of his life to give public voice to the question. Soon after the first public reading of this play, he was diagnosed with the cancer that attacked his brain and eventually took his life.

Had Lawrence Langer not introduced us to the concept of "choiceless choices" as a description of the victim's situation and of our own inability to make moral judgments regarding the victim's behavior in the world of the camps, Ziering's play would have insisted that we invent such language, that we confront a world in which such "choiceless choices" define the universe created by the perpetrator for the victims. Langer reiterates the statement of Andrzej Wirth, who commented on Tadeusz Borowski's work *This Way to the Gas, Ladies and Gentlemen*, "The tragedy lies not in the necessity of choosing, but in the impossibility of making a choice." Choiceless choices, Langer understands—and Ziering so keenly illustrates—do not reflect options between good and bad, life and death but between one form of abnormal response and another, both impossible, imposed by a situation not of the victim's own choosing.

So we must caution ourselves that Bierhoff did not create the circumstances his daughter Ellen faced, he merely had to act under the most circumscribed conditions. He loved his daughter, he murdered his daughter, he assumed the responsibility of alleviating the pain that she would face on the morrow. Even his fate—execution by the perpetrator for his callousness—merely underscores the depth of his victimization. Kommandant Roschmann utters the final words that Herman hears:

> "You Jewish pig, you child murderer. The Fuehrer is right: you Jews are nothing but an inferior race without any morals." A shot is fired and in all innocence the kommandant give his instructions: "It is absolutely essential that you make sure no children are left behind in today's Action, in order to prevent further killings of innocent children by these damned Jews."

Naturally, Ziering seeks wisdom from the precedents of previous Jewish history: the *Akeidah*, the Binding of Isaac, which was the name the rabbis gave to the what the Torah describes as the "Test of Abraham"; the Crusades when loving fathers slew their sons and merciful mothers their daughters lest they be forcibly converted to Christianity, when entire communities chose to "sanctify God's name"; and the Zealots of Masada who chose suicide over surrender to the Romans. They would not compromise their political freedom. They acted on the ethic that Patrick Henry would later proclaim, "Give me *liberty* or give me death."

But the Holocaust is without precedent and it is difficult to impose the wisdom of precedents on an experience that is so singular within history. Jews were not martyrs but victims. They did not die *al kiddush hashem* [for the sanctification of the Divine Name]. The pious were killed alongside those whose ancestors had converted, those who were without belief, or who had no knowledge of or allegiance to Jewish tradition. The rabbis who attempted to apply the precedents of *halachah*, of Jewish law, to their decisions failed, as did their colleagues who approached the issue of theodicy through the prism of earlier Jewish theology and proclaimed: "Because of our sins, we were exiled from the land." For God to remain just, they must blame the victim for their victimization and insist that the annihilation of six million Jews of Europe was worthy of the divine pedagogue. This theology may have worked as Jews grappled with the destruction of the first and second Temples in 586 B.C.E. and 70 C.E. respectively, but the evil of the Holocaust is so disproportionate that Richard L. Rubenstein is right when he refused to accept it as applicable to the annihilation of European Jewry. To see Hitler as the instrumentality of God is offensive. Any God worthy of being God surely must have a better way to instruct and admonish a people.

A few rabbis in the *Shoah*, such as Rabbis Yitzhak Nissenbaum and Yissachar Shlomo Teichthal, and several Jewish theologians, writers and artists after the Shoah, understood that unprecedented times imposed the creation of a new language. One merely has to view Samuel Bak's *Landscapes of the Jewish Experience* or *In A Different Light* to understand the requirements of such a language.

As to the *Akeidah*, problematic as it is, the test of Abraham was only a test, a demonstration of fidelity to God, and a willingness to sacrifice all to demonstrate a steadfastness of commitment to the One. In the Biblical narrative Isaac survives—a ram is offered in his stead—and ever since then symbolic offerings replaced human sacrifice in Jewish tradition. Ellen does not survive. This is no test. No act of witness is required. In contemporary Israeli writing, more attention is paid to Isaac, who is treated as the first survivor, the man who saw death face-to-face and survived to then marry, raise children and found a dynasty. The Biblical account is scarce as to details of Isaac after the *Akeidah*. He does not return with his father. He is not present at his mother's funeral. He is next seen when he greets his bride at the age of 40, which depending on his age at the time of the test is according to rabbinic legend, three, 27 or 37 years after he saw his father raise his arm to slay him. Isaac's inability to see at the end of his life is surely not unrelated to what he saw at the beginning.

Those Jews who offered their children in the Crusades rather than abandon their faith killed for a purpose; their children died for a purpose. The Nazis martyred Jehovah's Witnesses. All they had to do was to sign a document denouncing their faith in order to be released from prison. Herbert Bierhoff did not offer Ellen as a sacrifice. No martyr, she was but another of the Nazis' many victims. There was no call from on high. God was absent, not even a divine tear was shed. And thus her death at the hands of her loving father is an atrocity, no less unsettling and far more perplexing than her death would have been at the hands of the Germans.

And Herman Bierhoff was no zealot. He was choosing between one form of death and another more brutal, more torturous death. There was no freedom at the end of the trial. He was not, as the fighters in the Warsaw Ghetto Uprising, making a last stand, a final gesture of honor.

He was simply protecting his daughter from a fate worse than immediate death—or so he thought.

Judge Herbert? No! Judge the killers. They created the situation in which loving fathers murdered their daughters as an act of mercy and grace.

Judge God – for any act so absolute is ultimate. It indicts divinity as well as humanity. It shatters both and it haunts those who live in its aftermath.

Above all, judge the perpetrators.

Still, explicitly or implicitly each of the survivors judge God. An event so absolute always pushes toward ultimacy. For Ruth who imposed this burden on Shimon by recounting her dream, Abraham pleaded for mercy but God remained silent throughout. Shimon's God is also silent. God cannot judge or will not judge. Satan is mocking God for human evil. For Esther, a survivor whose guidance Shimon sought, the loss of God is as dangerous as belief in God. Without God, there are no limits. She understands Dostoyevski. If God is dead, everything is permissible —even Auschwitz.

Had not Irving Greenberg first introduced us the paradox of the Holocaust—that the innocent feel guilty and the guilty feel innocent— we would have learned it from *The Judgment of Herbert Bierhoff.* There is a vast literature of survivor guilt to which Ziering's work is a significant addition, but only the barest of literature regarding the guilt of the perpetrators by the perpetrators. Where it exists, that literature is usually written by non-perpetrators, those inquiring as to their motives and their sense of responsibility. The grandchildren of the perpetrators feel guilty. They flock to films such as *Schindler's List.* They read Daniel Jonah Goldhagen's *Hitler's Willing Executioners* in English before it was translated into German and became a bestseller. They stayed on late into the evening—even unto dawn—discussing the guilt of the German people and their role as Hitler's henchmen. Rejected by many critics because it was too blanket an indictment of the German nation, because it stereotyped the Germans without considering diverse motivations and personal struggles with conscience, Goldhagen's work was embraced by German youth who asked uncompromising questions of their grandparents—questions their parent's were too polite to ask and their grandparents would have preferred had never been asked.

In Act II, Scene 6, Ziering depicts the technical answers of German judges, prosecutors and defense attorneys convened by the German consulate in 1980. They are without insight, without depth. I suspect we all would be surprised by the new generation. It holds greater promise.

Elie Wiesel has written that, "Only those who were there will ever know and those who were there can never tell." Over the years as I have studied the Holocaust, I have found it prudent to respect the first of Wiesel's insights and imperative to reject the second. While I may know more about the Holocaust—more about the history, psychology, theology and philosophy—survivors have a sense of being there that must be respected. We must learn to listen in order to understand what is being told. That which is revealed may hide that which is concealed as every student of Torah or of psychology soon learns and the process of revelation conceals as it reveals, but the act of telling by a survivor must be treated with respect. But we cannot *ab initio* negate the possibility of telling, certainly not now when so many efforts have been made to tell and a new generation is prepared, perhaps as never before, to listen.

For Esther, telling is all that the survivor can do. Telling may not lead to understanding, but it can at least deepen the question: "We are all alive; we all raised families with children and grandchildren. Therefore we have made optimistic, pro-life decisions in spite of our experience whether rational or not. Our function is simply to record and tell in a factual way without embellishments our personal experiences and the events which we witnessed." Whether that leads to understanding, she does not tell. But it imposes yet another responsibility on the survivors, one they have discharged with great intensity in recent years.

On some level, Ziering indicates that they fear such understanding for it might involve acceptance. Hannah Arendt once wrote:

> "Comprehension does not mean denying the outrageous, deducing the unprecedented from precedence, or explaining phenomena by such analogies and generalities that the impact of reality and the shock of experience are no longer felt. It means, rather, examining and bearing consciously the burden, which our century [the 20th century] has placed on us—neither denying its existence nor submitting meekly to its weight."[1]

---

[1] Hannah Arendt, *The Origins of Totalitarianism* (New York: World, 1951), viii.

But understanding is only possible now.

Shimon says: "Look, as teenagers we rarely asked such questions. We reacted both literally and figuratively solely from our gut instinct. Had we pondered then the question of why, most likely like many in the older generation we would have either chosen suicide or sunk to the sorry state of *Muselman*, the walking ghosts in the camps—with no chance of surviving."

No one confronts these questions without paying a price. Survivors all know it about each other. The scholars who grapple with the Holocaust also know it about each other. We can discern those who have long struggled with these issues from those who are new or merely treat it in passing.

Only at a distance can understanding be achieved. Ziering is acutely conscious and makes the reader aware again and again that he had reached the years of a man's life, three score and ten, and it was time to confront that past. And the question that he left us with will haunt all who read his work.

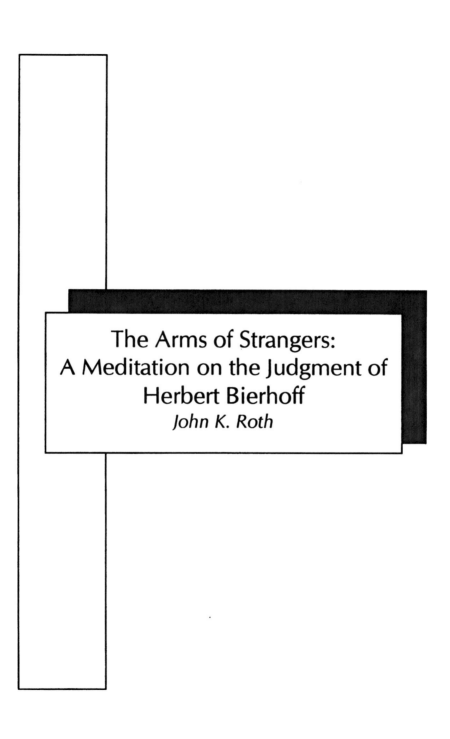

The Arms of Strangers:
A Meditation on the Judgment of
Herbert Bierhoff
John K. Roth

The Arms of Strangers

Give us God, the evening,
the evening,
the good evening
Thus a cheerful morning.

—"Ky_era, Ky_era," a children's song
from *Into the Arms of Strangers*

In early September 2000, my good friend Michael Berenbaum, the editor of these reflections about Sigi Ziering's *The Judgment of Herbert Bierhoff*, invited me to a Warner Bros. premiere in Hollywood, California. The film we saw that night was a special documentary about the *Kindertransport* (children's transports) program, an aspect of the Holocaust that has received too little attention. Thanks to the dedication of Deborah Oppenheimer, the film's producer, that situation will change for the better. *Into the Arms of Strangers* draws on oral history and evocative film footage that are amplified by a moving soundtrack based on children's songs from the period. In moving and personal ways, it focuses on the period between November 1938 and the beginning of World War II in September 1939. During that window of opportunity, 9,354 Jewish children were evacuated to Britain from areas under Nazi control. Assisted primarily by the Refugee Children's Committee, a private

British organization, those unaccompanied girls and boys found a safe haven from the Holocaust that was about to sweep through Europe and scar the earth forever.

Oppenheimer's mother, Sylvia Avramovici Oppenheimer, was among the German Jewish children who found a haven in England when, shortly after Sylvia's eleventh birthday, her parents were able to send her there in August 1939, only days before the final train left Berlin on the last day of that month. At the time, the so-called "Final Solution of the Jewish question" had not yet unleashed mass murder in German-occupied Europe. Forced emigration remained the official Nazi policy for Jews under the swastika. Unfortunately, antisemitism and fears about economic competition in circumstances still affected by the Great Depression meant that few places were interested in Jewish refugees, especially if the refugees were adults. For a few months in 1938-1939, however, the situation was slightly better for several thousand Jewish children between the ages of seven and sixteen. In the United Kingdom, though not in the United States where welcoming legislation was initiated but blocked in Congress, a combination of private initiative, governmental support, and British generosity opened doors to safety for Jewish boys and girls when, less than two weeks after the November pogroms that the Germans euphemistically called *Kristallnacht*, Parliament announced its decision on November 21, 1938: England would permit "an unspecified number of children up to age seventeen from German-occupied lands to enter the United Kingdom as 'transmigrants.'" The stories about those children and their families—including the British families who sheltered and adopted them—are bittersweet. Like Deborah Oppenheimer's mother, most of the rescued Jewish children never saw their parents again.

As the film's title suggests, the parting of parent and child in the Third Reich's railroad stations was heartbreaking. Parents were sending their children into the arms of strangers, but Jewish families had to make that "choiceless choice," to use the Holocaust scholar Lawrence L. Langer's phrase, because the chances for a normal Jewish life in Germany had all but disappeared once *Kristallnacht* had taken place. Uncertainty, anguish, and fear pervaded the partings. Parents reassured their children that the separation would not last long, and no doubt children sometimes did the same for their mothers and fathers. But on all sides, those hopes and wishes often disguised the fact that the future for these Jewish families was scarcely good. In one of the film's most gripping moments, a Holocaust survivor relates that her father, unable to stand the parting, snatched her from the *Kindertransport* as the train departed from Germany. The father did not survive the Holocaust. His daughter came through the onslaught only after enduring numerous Nazi camps, including Auschwitz.

The *Kindertransport* program meant life for the precious few who qualified for its benefits, but no words can express the incalculably high price paid for that rescue. Nevertheless, the price includes terror and grief that can be at least partially felt by anyone who has even momentarily contemplated what it would be like to give up a dearly loved child—not knowing where or to whom the child may be going—or who might try to imagine a child's feelings when dearly loved parents are sending her or him away alone. For this reason, *Into the Arms of Strangers* is a film about the Holocaust that may presently be unrivaled in its ability to use history's particularity to communicate key aspects of the Holocaust's universal significance.

The Holocaust's core included the destruction of the Jewish family, which was and is essential for the vitality of Jewish life. Ironically, however, even the *Kindertransport* program was not entirely at odds with Nazi objectives, for it broke up families and removed Jewish children from the Reich. Nor was the British welcome entirely free of problematic compromise. It was arguable an understandable legal provision that the Jewish children were to be received in England on a temporary basis, for, among other things, it was probably assumed—disastrously mistaken though that belief turned out to be—that they would be reunited with their parents on the continent. It was honorable that British sterling in an amount exceeding 500,000 pounds was quickly raised to cover the fifty-pound bond that Britain required for each Jewish child. Yet it remained true that the children's parents were not welcomed for fear that they would become unwelcome job competitors or burdens on the state. The *Kindertransport* program was a blessing but not one that was unmixed. Thus, gratitude for the rescue of those Jewish children must combine with resistance to combat anything akin to the arrogantly antisemitic and racist forces or the exclusionary, family-separating refugee policies that required the *Kindertransport*'s "choiceless choices" to be made at all. Otherwise the gratitude becomes sentimentality that does little to prevent or halt the genocidal destruction of families that remains a haunting threat after the Holocaust.

The Judgment of Herbert Bierhoff and *Into the Arms of Strangers* make strong companion pieces, for Ziering's "judgement" embraces "the arms of strangers," albeit in even more wrenching ways than Oppenheimer's documentary emphasizes. In her film, the strangers' arms were largely welcoming and friendly; they saved the lives of Jewish children. In his play, which is also based on actual events, the strangers' arms are hostile and murderous. They embody an escalation and radicalization of Nazi policy that went far beyond the *Kindertransport* program's prewar months. The escalation and radicalization extended to the eastern European ghettos and killing centers that stood at the center of Nazi Germany's full-fledged effort to destroy the Jewish people. In Riga, Latvia, for example, the Nazi-established Jewish ghetto was in more ways than one far removed from Britain and the safety that country gave to the Kindertransportees. Especially in 1943, no Jewish child was safe in Riga. There, parents faced "choiceless choices" of a kind that would scarcely have been imaginable even in August 1939 when Deborah Oppenheimer's mother said goodbye to her parents, departed Germany, and found a life very different from the one her parents had once envisioned for her.

German forces occupied the Baltic state of Latvia and Riga, its capital city, during the summer of 1941. With the help of local collaborators, the Germans had killed about 90 percent of the country's 95,000 Jews by the end of that year, including most of the approximately 30,000 Latvian Jews who were initially confined in the Riga ghetto. The clearing of that ghetto made its space available to concentrate Jews who were deported eastward from Germany and Austria during the winter of 1941-1942. By November 1943, the Riga ghetto had been "liquidated" as part of Nazi Germany's genocidal campaign to make Europe *Jüdenrein*.

Ziering's narrative about the Bierhoff family reflects this history. The Bierhoff's—Herbert, Ruth, and their daughter Ellen, who was not yet six in the early autumn of 1943—were German Jews. They were deported from Kassel, their hometown, to Riga on December 9, 1941. Back in the prewar months of 1939, Ellen Bierhoff would have been much too young for the *Kindertransport* program. In 1943, however, her parents had successfully hidden her from the "selections" that were rapidly thinning the Riga ghetto's already reduced population as the Germans' collapsing eastern military front led them to kill the remaining Jews or to relocate those who could still be exploited as slave laborers. An "unproductive" Jewish child, Ellen Bierhoff was worse than useless to the Germans in Riga during the autumn of 1943. Hiding was unlikely to save her life much longer. No *Kindertransport*'s deliverance awaited her family, but "choiceless choices" did. Ziering makes his audience consider the unbearable dilemmas that Nazi domination forced on the Bierhoff family. If that responsibility gives his audience more than it can bear, one can scarcely imagine what the actual circumstances must have been for Herbert, Ruth, and Ellen, their precious child.

The cast of Ziering's play includes a survivor named David who sums up what happened. As a member of the Jewish ghetto police, Herbert Bierhoff knew that the Nazis were about to launch yet another *Aktion* to murder more of the Riga ghetto's diminished Jewish population. Ellen would surely fall into the brutal and murderous arms of Nazi strangers. Bierhoff would be unable to save her. He faced a decision that no parent should ever have to consider. Ellen's father, David tells us, "chose the only way open to him, the mercy killing of his beloved daughter, in order to avoid an infinitely more brutal killing by the SS."

Before he had given his daughter the poison that killed her, Bierhoff did what fathers often do. With reassuring words spoken to give a child comfort in her particular circumstances—"tomorrow you are going on a trip where you'll have many oranges, and all the food you can eat"—he said good night to Ellen. It was the last time he would do so. It was not even his fate to remember that night for long, because when the Germans discovered what he had done to Ellen, they shot him dead. Meanwhile, Ruth survived her daughter and husband, but not the Holocaust. Her experiences in the Riga ghetto were too much to bear. As she lay dying, she charged Shimon, the Bierhoffs' friend, to find "competent judges who will declare that Herbert was merciful and right in giving Ellen the pill." Part of the Holocaust's oral testimony, this wrenching story came to Ziering, whose play and cast put Herbert Bierhoff's heartbreaking dilemma before us.

Was Herbert Bierhoff merciful and right when he gave Ellen that pill? The survivor named David says yes. Kurt, another survivor, is not so sure. There was always the chance, somehow, that Ellen might survive. Stranger things happened in the Holocaust. Kurt also wonders why Ellen's father did not take his own life after he took hers. In addition, there is the question of whether Herbert Bierhoff should have consulted with Ruth, his wife, before he took the decision that he seems to have made alone. Esther, a third survivor, listens to David and Kurt. She feels the dilemma's agony, but she has fewer "answers" than the men. Rejecting closure, she emphasizes that the survivors should simply "record and tell in a factual way, without embellishments, our personal experiences and the events which we witnessed." Sigi Ziering gives the play's last word to Shimon, the survivor who seeks to fulfill Ruth Bierhoff's last wish. Herbert Bierhoff, says Shimon, "did the right thing." But then Shimon pauses and delivers the last line: "Or did he?" *The Judgment of Herbert Bierhoff* asks us to consider the judgement that a Jewish father made and then to make a judgement about his decision. How can we accept this challenge? How can we not?

All of the main points in the paragraph above have a place in the response I want to make to Shimon's hard question: "Or did he?" First and foremost, I think there is no closure, at least none that I can or should attempt to provide. If I jump to a conclusion, I do not allow the Bierhoffs' anguish to be fully expressed, for full expression requires not only a giving of testimony but a receiving of it as well. Ziering's play tells an unsettled story. It is not for me to "settle" what should remain unsettling.

That said, I acknowledge that Ellen, somehow, might have survived, but I also believe that Herbert Bierhoff acted out of love that was driven by the desperation of the "choiceless choice" he faced. As Lawrence Langer defines the concept, a "choiceless choice" is neither normal nor made in circumstances of one's own choosing. Such choices are forced and between options that are unacceptable or worse. Therefore, I do not say that Bierhoff did the "right" thing, and certainly I do not say that he did a "good" thing. The words *right* and *good* can scarcely apply in the situation that the Bierhoff family faced, which was definitely not of their own choosing. One can say, I believe, that Ellen's father acted out of fatherly love, which was determined not to let his daughter fall into the arms of strangers who were hellbent on her destruction. In that sense, as a Jewish father committed to the best he could do for his priceless daughter in the Riga ghetto during the autumn of 1943, Herbert Bierhoff may have had but one loving choice—choiceless though it was—once the option of poisoning his child to death presented itself in those unrelentingly brutal circumstances.

I wonder about Ruth. I tend to think that Herbert should have shared his intentions and obtained Ruth's consent, if not her help, in taking their daughter's life. But of that I am far less sure than of the moral fact that looms the largest in Ziering's play. That fact does not pertain primarily to the decisions Jews had to take in the Riga ghetto but to the decisions that Germans made in establishing that place and the murderous policies that governed it. Those decisions and policies were wrong—or nothing could be. Ziering's play focuses attention on the anguished "choiceless choices" of the Bierhoff family and countless other Jewish families during the Holocaust. That focus, crucial though it is, will be misplaced unless it motivates post-Holocaust audiences to resist the ideologies and conditions, the leaders and followers, that may again bring about conditions that require parents and children to confront dilemmas like the Bierhoffs encountered in the Riga ghetto or the Oppenheimers faced as the last trains of the *Kindertransport* were organized in August 1939.

Among the touching children's songs that form the soundtrack for *Into the Arms of Strangers*, there is a simple prayer sung in Czech by a young boy. It is a prayer that loving parents might teach a child to say as darkness falls. It is a song that a loving mother or father might sing to a young son or a daughter before sleep overtakes them. "Give us God, the evening," the words ask, "the evening, the good evening, [and] thus a cheerful morning." For Jewish parents and children during the Holocaust, good evenings and cheerful mornings were few and far between. That fact leaves us to ask: Where was God and where was humankind? In relatively small but still immensely important ways, the *Kindertransport* and its welcoming arms made the Holocaust's devastation in the Riga ghetto and elsewhere less than complete. Nevertheless, Ziering's play rightly keeps the focus on the devastation by drawing us into the anguish of the Bierhoffs, one particular Jewish family. One result of that anguish and of *The Judgment of Herbert Bierhoff* deserves to be a deliberate rage, a determined anger that commits one to resist any conditions like those that made the *Kindertransport* program necessary and the life of Ellen Bierhoff impossible.

Standing in Awe
Eugene Fisher

Reading this powerful and thought-provoking drama brought to mind the words of my colleague, Fr. John Hotchkin, who took up the "compelling need" for the Catholic Church to preserve the memory of the *Shoah* and to confront its implications for Catholic teaching in a memo addressed to the American bishops. He observed that, "the chillingly systematic effort to exterminate an entire people, not for what they had done nor for any threat they posed, but simply for being who they were—whether young or old; every last man, woman, and child—is an attempt at evil on a nearly unimaginable scale. Thus the *Shoah* raises in a most awful way the darkest questions the mystery of evil has put to the human family in our time. We may never get to the bottom of these questions. For something this evil there is in the end no explanation the mind can accept. It remains a dark and threatening mystery. But what we cannot explain, we must nevertheless remember. The warning contained in the memory is our best common shield and defense. The evil that turns humanity against humanity, cheapening its life, degrading it, bent on its destruction, still lurks in the world. It does not rest and neither must we in our remembering, for it is by remembering the unspeakable horror that did in fact happen that we remain awake and alert to the possibility that what happened could be attempted again. It is through our common remembrance of those who perished that they shield the living. This is a cataclysm unlike any other in human history. Indeed, the theologian David Tracy has written of it as an "interruption" of history, an event in which "our history crashes against itself." It is as if time stopped, and history thereafter could never again be the same. For this reason it is imperative that the memory be kept and the story be told from generation to generation."[1]

Sigi Ziering's drama also reminds us of the precious witness of the survivors. As Pope John Paul II said in addressing the remnant of the Jewish community of Warsaw, "Today the people of Israel, perhaps more than ever before, finds itself at the center of the attention of the nations of the world, above all because of this terrible experience, through which you have become a warning voice for all humanity, for all nations, all the powers of the world, all systems and every person. More than anyone else, it is precisely you who have become this saving warning. I think that in this sense you continue your particular vocation, showing yourselves to be still heirs of that election to which God is faithful. This is your mission in the contemporary world before the peoples, the nations, all of humanity, the Church. And in this Church all peoples and nations feel united to you in this mission."[2]

The above reflections frame my attitude of profound respect for victims and survivors as I strive to make a coherent comment on only a few of the many moral and spiritual issues raised in this drama. My first is that of course no human being can, really, sit on judgment on Herbert Bierhoff. One would need the total knowledge only God can possess of the soul of a human being to even begin such a process. My own guess is that if there is such a divine judgment the verdict can only be "innocent." In Catholic theology, which like Jewish thought has a long history of dealing with imponderables and paradoxes, there is a distinction that leads me to the above speculation. This is the distinction between objective wrong and subjective guilt. A person can commit an act that is in itself

[1] As cited by Archbishop Alexander Brunett in the introduction to *Catholics Remember the Holocaust* (Washington, D.C.: National Conference of Catholic Bishops, 1998). The volume gathers together statements on the Shoah issued by the bishops' conferences of Hungary, Germany, Poland, the U.S., Holland, Switzerland, France and Italy from 1994 to 1998, and the Holy See's *We Remember: A Reflection on the Shoah.*

[2] June 14, 1987, cited in Eugene Fisher and Leon Klenicki, editors, *Spiritual Pilgrimage: Pope John Paul II on Jews and Judaism 1979-1995* (New York: Crossroad, 1995).

sinful, according to Catholic tradition, without committing a sin. To commit a sin, one must knowingly choose evil. Here, the moral universe inhabited by Herbert Bierhoff has been so perverted by the massive triumph of pure evil that an individual like Bierhoff can be—and I would argue was—rendered bereft of the moral freedom necessary to make a meaningful choice between good and evil. There simply was no morally "good" option open to him, subjectively. He is innocent of any guilt. A victim, not in any sense a perpetrator.

Saying this, I would note that also according to Catholic tradition (as I understand it—please remember that I am not a professional moral theologian by any means!), there can be no excuse for the taking of innocent human life. In the "objective" order, what happened was murder, clearly and indefensibly. No one has a moral "right" to arrogate to him or herself what is proper to the role of the Author of Life. In this sense every murder is a blasphemy. And if one takes seriously the notion that every human person is created in and as God's image, every murder borders on deicide.[3]

There are, for Catholics, no real exceptions to the commandment, "Thou Shalt Not Murder," understood as the direct taking of innocent human life. Self defense and the just war theory are based on the notion that someone or some group out to murder me and mine do not fall under the category of "innocence." Thus, from the point one considers embryonic human life to be human life, there can be no exceptions to the prohibition of direct acts of abortion.[4] Nor can euthanasia, however glossed over as a "quality of life" issue or "doctor assisted suicide" ever be condoned. They are the murder of innocents.

As the father of a lovely little girl, I found myself trapped in Bierhoff's impossible dilemma. Logically, "objectively," I found myself saying "let her live," maybe there is a chance she will survive. Others did. Subjectively (and the subjective was the only reality open to Bierhoff, of course, as it

---

[3] The irony here that so many Christians persecuted and murdered Jews over the centuries out of the perverted belief that "the Jews" were a "deicide" people should not be passed over in silence in Christian religious education courses.

[4] Some indirect acts that could have the "double effect" of aborting a fetus though intended to have a principal curative effect are allowable. But to delve into this the reader would be well advised to take a course at his or her local Catholic college taught by a competent moral theologian.

is to any of us), I found myself simply overwhelmed. Morally frozen. I have read too much, heard the testimony of too many survivors, to be at this stage of my life vain enough to think that I can, through logic, derive satisfying answers to the questions most survivors, and certainly this play, pose to all humanity. I can only affirm the moral "rightness" of Sigi Ziering's questions, and stand in awe before the persistence and moral courage he shows in continuing to ask them on behalf of all humanity. This is "prophetic witness," indeed, as the Pope said, and in learning to listen to it, we open ourselves as Christians to it as a "saving warning" for us all. I trust it will be taken as a mark of respect if I say that, for me, both the protagonists of the play and its author in their unceasing wrestling with the mystery of evil are true martyrs, each in his own sense, for *HaShem*, the One God, who called Israel to wrestle with His Own Mystery.

Ziering includes in his dialogue a number of insights, each worthy of volumes of reflection by the best thinkers ours and future generations can provide. The author, for example, gives to Esther the line: "But what frightens me even more than the realization that there might not be a God after Auschwitz is the fact of what a godless society is capable of, based on our camp experiences." This thought alone could and should become the theme of countless scholarly conferences and local, congregational level dialogues between Jews and Christians.

At one point, he notes almost in passing that "what happened in Germany could not have happened in Denmark, in Holland or in Bulgaria, to name just a few countries." This can be true only in the past tense, since as John Hotchkin noted, the overwhelming power of evil revealed to us in the *Shoah* must never be underestimated. No human society is immune.

Still, Shimon is quite right historically. I would add Catholic Italy to the list of places where it "could not have happened," and Catholic Austria to places where it did happen. The Nazi goal, as Yitz Greenberg has pointed out, was the same in all of German-occupied countries: total annihilation of all Jews. At least two major factors differed from place to place, however. The first was the general social attitude of the majority population toward its Jewish fellow-citizens. The Italians, the Danes and the Bulgarians simply did not view their neighbors through a "racial" lens and so could not be "sold" on the racial ideology that lay at the very heart of Nazism.[5] Persisting in seeing their neighbors as fully human themselves, despite Nazi propaganda, they acted accordingly.

The second factor derives directly from Nazi racial ideology. Different groups, in Nazi eyes, occupied distinct strata on the way to full, Aryan humanity. The Dutch and the Danes, like the Germans themselves, were considered fully human. Slavs and others occupied descending strata down to creatures such as Jews, Roma, and Africans, which were impure vermin that needed to be "cleansed" from the body of the new humanity fit to inherit the millennial "thousand year reign (Reich)" envisioned in Nazi eschatology. Slavs, a middle category, might be fit for slavery, but no more, and only those most "Aryan-like." The occupation of Poland, therefore, differed qualitatively from the occupation of Denmark or Holland. No attempt was made to establish even a fictitious collaborationist government. Anyone who might be or become a leader was ruthlessly hunted down, including thousands of Catholic clergy. To help a Jew in even the smallest way was a capital crime, often swiftly and brutally carried out. Thus, playing any sort of "numbers game" comparing how many Jews survived in this society or that society, and using that to compare the societies themselves is at best far more complex than any scholars have attempted thus far, and at worst a bizarre attempt that ironically apes the category judgments of the German occupiers themselves. What was done can only be measured by what could have been done, and the Nazis changed the rules and therefore the possibilities country by country and in some cases region by region within the same country.[6]

---

[5] The centrality of Nazism's racial ideology, and its consequent desire to re-fashion human nature itself, of course, was one of the key factors distinguishing Nazism on the historically earlier totalitarian systems of Spanish and Italian fascism on which Nazism was to some extent modeled. It has been argued that one of the great mistakes made by many otherwise astute political leaders in Europe in the early 1930's was to see Nazism as simply another form of fascism, leading many both inside and outside of Germany to a fatal underestimation of the reality of Nazism's stated goals.

[6] I have seen, for example, Catholic apologists arguing that Catholicism insulated its people against Nazi racial ideology more successfully than Protestantism (thus implying the superiority of Catholic over Reformation theology)—and other authors, presumably Protestant but in one case Jewish, arguing exactly the

In this context, a point might be at least tentatively raised for consideration in the Jewish-Christian dialogue that perhaps deserves more concerted attention. It is very clear, on the one hand, that the ancient Christian "teaching of contempt" against Jews and Judaism is causally related to the Holocaust. Without it, one cannot explain why so may Europeans so easily accepted Nazi racial ideology to the point of acting on it to become willing perpetrators or knowing bystanders in genocide.[7] On the other hand, numerous studies have shown that there was no real, qualitative difference in the teaching of contempt between Protestant, Catholic and Orthodox religious teaching of the period, and the centuries which lead up to it. Likewise, what a young Catholic in Austria would have learned about Jews and Judaism in catechism classes would have been virtually indistinguishable from what young Italians would have learned. Yet, place, society and culture did matter. It made a difference, often a great difference in survival, whether one was a Jew in Denmark or in Austria or in Bulgaria. Evidently, religion

---

opposite. In both cases, the deck is carefully stacked with examples drawn from the countries with the most successful rescue ratios of one religious tradition pitted against countries of the other religious tradition with lower percentages of Jews saved. In either case, to my mind, such comparisons are invidious. It is morally loathsome to attempt to use a body count of Jewish victims to prove the "superiority" of one branch of Christianity over another. There is more than sufficient guilt for all Christians to repent.

[7] There is another category that I believe should be used along with the now-classic "perpetrators, bystanders, and rescuers." It is a subcategory of "bystanders," but brings out what I believe is at least arguably an important distinction. This would be something like "helpless bystanders," i.e., those who really could not have done anything but were not callously indifferent, just adrift themselves in the vast cataclysm that was World War II. Some might not have had the opportunity, given their place and time, though would have if a Jew had knocked on their door. Some might have been paralyzed in their own version of the lack of moral options faced by Herbert Bierhoff in the play. That is, for example, they had children themselves and lived in a place where the German occupiers habitually murdered the entire family of would-be rescuers. It is a moral decision on one level to risk one's own life to save someone. It is an altogether different moral question to risk the lives of one's family. That is a hard, hard moral dilemma that I, for one, would not like to face. I would like to think that I would be among the rescuers of Jews anyway. But it could be the luxury of not having to face the choice that is speaking for me.

alone cannot explain the virulence of racial antisemitism in a given society. Other factors are needed. Christian anti-Judaism, in this sense, was a *sine qua non* of the Holocaust, a "necessary cause." But it was not a sufficient cause.[8] More, perhaps much more, is needed to analyze the seeds of the *Shoah* on a country by country basis.

Archbishop Brunett, in his introduction cited above, draws out three essential reasons for Christians to remember the *Shoah*, and to include it in the core curriculum of all Catholic education:

1. There exists a close spiritual bond of faith that links Christians to the Jews.

2. Many Christians were involved in the events of this catastrophe, some as fellow victims, some as rescuers, but too many others sadly as bystanders or perpetrators. As Christians we are all linked together in the Church, not only with the goodness of saints but also with the failures of sinners.

3. One cannot overstate the abiding need to preserve the memory of the event itself as a warning for future generations.[9]

Archbishop Brunett continued with a reflection that I believe is quite pertinent for Christian readers of *The Judgment of Herbert Bierhoff:*

---

[8] The notion that Christian anti-Judaism was a *necessary cause* leading to the Holocaust, but not a *sufficient cause* was first made, to my knowledge, by then Harvard historian Yosef Hayim Yerushalmi in 1973, at one of the first major Jewish-Christian conferences on the subject. Eva Fleischner edited the papers from that conference under the title, *Auschwitz: Beginning of a New Era?* (New York: KTAV, Cathedral, ADL, 1977). Yerushalmi was arguing against Rosemary Reuther's theory "that genocide against the Jews was an inexorable consequence of Christian theological teaching." Yerushalmi responded that, "If it were, genocide should have come upon the Jews in the Middle Ages," when the Church had the power to carry through on its teachings in the public order. Citing medieval papal legislation protecting Jews, Yerushalmi argues that "the slaughter of Jews by the state was not part of the medieval Christian world-order. It became possible with the breakdown of that order." He notes that when the first statute of "purity of blood in Spain" was drawn up in Toledo in 1449, "it was immediately denounced by Pope Nicholas V, and its perpetrators were excommunicated," lamenting the lack of similar action by Pope Pius XI in 1935 when the Nuremberg laws were promulgated (pp. 103-4).

[9] *Catholics Remember the Holocaust,cit.,* 2.

"Sometimes our people ask whether the preservation of this memory pertains more to the Jewish people than to us since it is they who saw so many millions of their family members perish. Surely it must be realized that the death of these millions touches first of all the Jews with an immediacy that is specifically theirs. But the death of those who were taken represents a loss not only to their families, grave as that is, but a loss to the world that is incalculable. That alone is reason enough for all to mourn and to remember."[10]

What is stressed, each in its own way, by the specific statements of national bishops' conferences since 1994, is the sense of repentance ("*teshuvah*" as Cardinal Edward I. Cassidy put it so clearly on that dark, rainy day in 1990 when the International Catholic-Jewish Liaison Committee visited Theresienstadt, and as the Holy See's Commission for Religious Relations with the Jews put it in 1998). This is not necessarily a repentance of personal guilt on the part of all Catholics, many of whom were not even alive when the Shoah took place, and most of whose ancestors, as well, lived continents and oceans away from the actual events. But what Pope John Paul II and *We Remember* are calling on all of us as Catholics to do is to assume the requirement of repentance for a change of heart and a change of life. It is to turn away from the teaching of contempt and to turn toward Jews in dialogue rather than conversionism. It is to assume responsibility for the past, yes, but much more so for the future, so that together we Catholics can ensure that "never again" will such a horror, such an eruption of evil into human history be possible, against the Jews or any other people.

In order to implement the mandate of the Pope and the Holy See, Catholic educators will need to incorporate into their teaching not only a sense of the awesome evil of the *Shoah*, but also a vibrant sense of the stories of the rescuers. Young people need role models to aspire to, not just long lists of "don'ts." As Yosef Yerushalmi again wisely put it almost three decades ago: "I do not want Christians to brood on the guilt of

---

[10] *Ibidem.*

their forebears and to keep apologizing for it. . .Be it known, however, that not by your ancestors but by your actions will you be judged."[11]

Cardinal William H. Keeler, in contemplating the role of the rescuers in Catholic education at a ceremony honoring them at the United Stated Holocaust Memorial Museum in 1997, adduced three salient points about them that have emerged from scholarly studies of why they did what they did to save Jews:

1. Whether highly educated or "just folks", a sense of morality was "deeply implanted in the fiber of their being." This was vital since "they frequently had to make a life-or-death decision on very short notice— perhaps a matter of minutes." By and large, they have told interviewers, "they felt they had little choice but to rescue." How do we, today, imbue in our students this instinct for rescue?

2. Whether confessedly religious or not, "the righteous had a deep sense that there was ultimate meaning to life beyond the present." They felt there was significance to what they did or did not do in daily life, in all decisions, that transcended themselves. We Christians and Jews speak here of the critical importance of faith in God.

3. Many of the righteous had a prior acquaintance with Jews, though not necessarily with the ones they saved. Here we see the importance of programs introducing people to each other across religious, racial and ethnic boundaries.

Many of those who did not attempt to help their neighbors, it has been argued, saw Jews as "morally expendable." How can Catholic educators today convince our students that each and every human being is "indispensable," vital to all others, in a word, an image of God for each and every one of us?

---

[11] *Auschwitz: Beginning of a New Era?* 106-7.

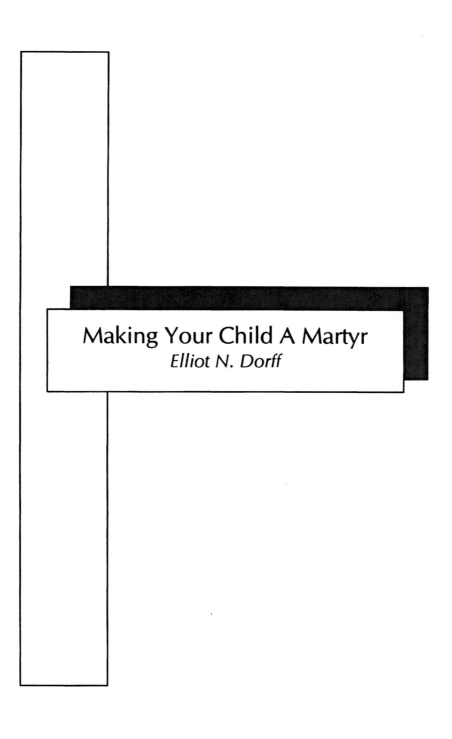

Making Your Child A Martyr
Elliot N. Dorff

Sigi Ziering's play, *The Judgment of Herbert Bierhoff*, raises a poignant question that many who suffered through the Holocaust faced: Do you kill your children rather than let the Nazis do that? Parents who chose that undoubtedly acted out of compassion, intending to provide their children with as quick and painless a death as possible within the familiar context of family rather than subject them to being wrenched from their families, humiliated, and murdered brutally in strange surroundings. But would Judaism condone such actions, as loving and protective as they were intended to be? If not, what *would* classical Jewish texts instruct parents faced with this situation to do?

Those questions are especially hard before the act, when parents ask their rabbi for a rabbinic ruling about what to do, but it is also wrenching after the fact, as presented in this play. Are parents who have killed their children under such circumstances to be considered merely murderers, with all the attendant guilt and shame involved in addition to whatever punishment may apply? Or are they to be considered saviors of their children's and Judaism's honor through an act of justified martyrdom?

Note that I am not dealing with the somewhat easier question—morally, not emotionally—of killing infants who cry and thereby undermine Jews' attempts to escape. That situation is also morally murky, but there the lives of others are at stake, a factor that argues for the moral rectitude of killing the child, while here no such justification exists. Furthermore, in Sigi Ziering's play, Ellen's existence threatens no one when her father, Herbert, gives her a pill to kill her before the Nazis presumably will.

Jewish Legal Rulings on Suicide and Martyrdom

All of these question correctly presume that Jewish law would normally prohibit both murder and suicide. The ban against murder, already announced in the Cain and Abel story in the opening chapters of Genesis, is legally ensconced in the Decalogue, announced amid thunder, lightning, and earthquakes atop Mount Sinai.[1] While the Torah itself articulates mitigating circumstances when the manslaughter occurred accidentally,[2] in the case Dr. Ziering's play describes and in many like it, the murder was clearly done in a conscious, premeditated manner. The murders involved, though, were not "with malice aforethought," and in that respect they are most akin to modern medical questions concerning assisted suicide (active euthanasia, "mercy killing"). In the latter case, though, the perpetrator contemplates murder in order to save a loved one from the physical pain of an illness, while in these cases the motive is to prevent either the physical pain of torture and its attendant risk of divulging information that would endanger others, the humiliation involved, or the forced desecration of the Jewish faith.

Jewish law on suicide emerged over centuries. The Midrash and Talmud[3] understand Genesis 9:5—"But for your own life-blood I [God] will require a reckoning"—as a ban against suicide, but the Bible records the suicides of Samson, Saul, and his armor bearer with no mention that they violated a law thereby. Indeed, later Jewish sources understand Saul's suicide as an act of martyrdom (*kiddush ha-shem*) "because he knew that the Philistines would do with him as they wished and put him to death."[4]

---

[1] Exodus 20:13. For the context of thunder, lightning, and earthquakes, see Exodus 19:16, 18.

[2] Exodus 21:13; Numbers 35:9-34.

[3] B. *Bava Kamma* 91b; *Genesis Rabbah* 34:13 (34:19 in some editions); cf. Mishnah Torah (M.T.) *Laws of Murder* 2:3; *Laws of the One Who Injures or Damages (Hovel u 'Mazik)* 5:1.

[4] Samson: Judges 16:30. Saul: I Samuel 31:4-5. See the evaluation of his suicide as permitted in Shulchan Aruch (S.A.) *Yoreh De'ah* 345:3 and the commentary of *Siftei Kohen* there.

They apply the same analysis to Hananiah, Mishael, and Azariah, where the claim to martyrdom is clearer, for, according to the Book of Daniel, they chose the fiery furnace rather than bow down to the statute of the king and his god, and they survived only through God's miraculous intervention.[5] Other Jewish sources also excuse the suicides of Saul and his armor bearer as acts done under duress.[6] Of the biblically recorded suicides it is only Ahitofel's that later Jewish sources deem unjustified, and they use that as the grounds for maintaining that "he who commits suicide while of sound mind has no share in the World to Come."[7]

Rabbinic literature presumes a ban against suicide but only once seems to articulate it—namely, in the passage cited above interpreting Genesis 9:5 to establish that prohibition. Aside from that, the Mishnah specifically forbids even injuring oneself, and the Talmud records Rabbi Hananyah ben Teradiyon's use of that principle in the context of suicide. While the Romans burned him at the stake for teaching Torah, he refuses to inhale the flames so that he might die faster, saying, "Better that God who gave life should take it; a person may not injure himself/herself."[8] Similarly, the Mishnah declares: "Against your will your were formed, against your will you were born, against your will you live, against your will you die, and against your will some day in the future you will have to give an accounting and a reckoning before the Ruler of Rulers, the Holy Blessed One."[9]

---

[6] Saul and his armor bearer: 1 Samuel 31:3-5; that it was an act under duress: S.A. *Yoreh De'ah* 345:3.; that it was to prevent an act of desecration of the Divine Name before Israel: *Sefer Hasidim*, chapter 723.

[7] Ahitofel's suicide: 2 Samuel 17:23. See Irving J. Rosenbaum, *The Holocaust and Halakhah* (New York: Ktav, 1976), p. 36 and p. 162, n. 21, for a discussion of the origins of this maxim about the burial of suicides, including those who base it on the story of Ahitofel. B. *Sanhedrin* 90a maintains that because of his suicide, Ahitofel has no share in the World to Come. The general rule that people who commit suicide with sound mind are to be buried outside the cemetery: M.T. *Laws of Mourning* 1:11; S.A. *Yoreh De'ah* 345:1—or at its edge: Responsum no. 763 of Rabbi Solomon ben Abraham Adret (the "Rashba", c. 1235 - c. 1310). It is also possible that, in addition to the biblical people mentioned, Zimri also committed suicide (I Kings 6:18).

[8] That one may not injure him/herself: M. *Bava Kamma* 8:6 (90b); cf. M.T. *Laws of Injury and Damage* 5:1. The story of Rabbi Hananyah ben Teradiyon: B. *Avodah Zarah* 18a; cf. S.A. *Yoreh De'ah* 339:1 (with gloss).

[9] M. *Avot (Ethics of the Fathers)* 4:21.

While these mishnaic and talmudic sources prohibiting self-injury presume that all the more one may not commit suicide, and while the Mishnah specifically says that "against your will you live," the general ban against suicide appears clearly for the first time in the post-talmudic tractate *Semahot*, and it is held to be Jewish law from then on.[10] Indeed, later sources consider suicide worse than murder, for, they maintain, while murder may be motivated by a desire for gain or by anger, a person who commits suicide can have no such motives. Those motives, of course, do not justify murder, but they explain it in ways that do not entail, as suicide does, denial of the doctrines of reward and punishment, the world to come, and the sovereignty of God.[11] Thus Jewish law prescribes that, in contrast to the funeral of any other Jew, even a murderer, no rites are to be performed in honor of a person who commits suicide, including a eulogy, although everything that pertains to respect for the mourners is permitted.[12] Normal funeral arrangements are disallowed, though, only when there is clear evidence that the person who committed suicide was of sound mind, and in recent centuries the slightest indication has been construed to be enough to establish that he or she was at least temporarily insane at the time.[13] With children who commit suicide, the presumption of insanity at the time is irrebuttable.[14]

---

[10] *Semahot* 2:1-5; cf. S.A. *Yoreh De'ah* 339:1. The Conservative Movement's Committee on Jewish Law and Standards has asserted that while life-support systems (even artificial nutrition and hydration) may be removed from a dying patient with no reasonable hope for cure, both suicide and assisted suicide violate Jewish law; see my responsum, "Assisted Suicide," and the statement of the Committee based on it in Kassel Abelson and David Fine, eds., *Responsa 1991-2000 of the Committee on Jewish Law and Standards of the Conservative Movement* (New York: Rabbinical Assembly, 2002), 379-399. On this topic generally, see "Suicide," *Encyclopedia Judaica* 15:489-491.

[11] See, for example, Yehiel M. Tuchinsky, *Gesher Ha-Hayyim* (Jerusalem: Solomon, 1947, 1960), vol. 1, 269-270 [Hebrew]. I translate that passage in my responsum on Assisted Suicide (see the previous note) on p. 387.

[12] M.T. *Laws of Mourning* 1:11; S. A. *Yoreh De'ah* 345:1. See *Semahot* 2:1.

[13] Tuchinsky, *Gesher Ha-Hayyim* (see n. 11), vol. 1, ch. 25, which also contains a full list of the laws regarding a suicide [Hebrew]. For earlier formulations of this excuse of insanity, see *Semahot* 2:2-3; M.T. *Laws of Courts (Sanhedrin)* 18:6.

[14] *Semahot* 2:4-5; S.A. *Yoreh De'ah* 345:3.

Attempted suicides, though, are indeed punished. The Talmud records a dispute on whether a person may inflict nonfatal injuries on him/herself. The law that emerges is that one may not do so but human courts should not punish those who do.[15] Rabbinic sources, though, indicate that God might punish anyone who attempts suicide,[16] and the Rabbis themselves reserve the right to impose disciplinary flogging in lieu of punishment, especially if there seems to be an epidemic of attempted suicides within the community.[17] This seems both harsh and counterproductive to us moderns, especially given our presumption that people attempting suicide are crying out for help and should get both psycho-social support and medications to combat the chemical imbalances that cause depression. Still, these rules bespeak the Rabbis' deep conviction that normally we do not have the right to commit suicide because that would be to destroy God's property (our bodies) and to diminish the presence of God in the world, as articulated in Genesis 9:5.

Suicide, however, must be sharply differentiated from martyrdom. The Talmud itself maintains that one should accept death or even kill oneself rather than commit three sins—murder, incest/adultery, or idolatry[18]—and that sets the stage for later Jewish law and practice regarding martyrdom. Specifically, if ten Jews are present and the enemy demands transgression of any of the Torah's laws to demonstrate apostasy, then the Jew must rather die than disobey that law, whatever it be; but if ten Jews are not present, then, except for the cardinal three sins listed above, the Jew should rather violate the law than die. In times when the entire community is being forced to abandon Judaism, though, Jews must choose death rather than abandon any of Judaism's laws or even its customs.[19]

Since the Torah also demands, though, that we "live by them [the commandments]," a commandment the Rabbis interpret to mean that we must do what we can to preserve our own lives and those of others, Maimonides considers it a violation of Jewish law for Jews to choose to die rather than violate the law in circumstances where the law permits them to

---

[15] The dispute: B. *Bava Kamma* 91b. The law: M. *Bava Kamma* 8:6; S.A. *Hoshen Mishpat* 420:31.

[16] T. *Bava Kamma* 9:31.

[17] M.T. *Laws of Murder* 2:4-5; 11:5; S.A. *Hoshen Mishpat* 427:10.

[18] B. *Sanhedrin* 74a; S.A. *Yoreh De'ah* 157.

[19] M. T. *Laws of the Foundations of the Torah* 5:3.

save themselves. Ashkenazi authorities, however, consider such voluntary martyrdom praiseworthy, undoubtedly because they sought to provide legal warrant for the way that Ashkenazi Jews responded to the Crusades.[20] Thus Rabbi Yomtov b. Abraham Ashbili ("Ritva," 1250-1330) writes in the name of Rabbi Jacob ben Meir ("Rabbeinu Tam," 1100-1171), who himself was barely saved from death at the hands of the Crusaders: "An Israelite who is afraid that he will be forced to abandon Judaism and violate its commandments and who kills himself is not denied any burial or mourning rites. This was the reason that during the persecutions [of the Crusades] fathers slaughtered their children with their own hands."[21] Indeed, long before the Crusades, the Tanna'im, rabbis of the first two centuries C.E. living under Roman persecution, described martyrdom as virtually an everyday occurrence:

Those who dwell in the Land of Israel risk their lives for the sake of the commandments:

"Why are you being led out to be decapitated?"

"Because I circumcised my son to be an Israelite."

"Why are you being led out to be burned?"

"Because I read the Torah."

"Why are you being led out to be crucified?"

"Because I ate unleavened bread [on Passover]."

"Why are you getting a hundred lashes?"

"Because I performed the ceremony of the palm branch (lulav) [on Sukkot, the Festival of Booths, obeying Leviticus 23:40]. These wounds caused me to be beloved by my Father in heaven."[22]

Jewish Stories on Suicide and Martyrdom

In addition to the biblical stories of suicide and rabbinic rulings on the topic from the post-talmudic period to modern times, several stories in Jewish sources have shaped Jewish consciousness on this issue and inevitably affect how Jews have and should deal with the issue raised by Sigi Ziering's play. Indeed, Ziering himself mentions three of them.

---

[20] M.T. *Laws of Foundations of the Torah* 5:1; cf. 5:4, 6; Tosafot on B. *Avodah Zarah* 18a, 27b, 54a.

[21] Ritva, in his comments to B. *Avodah Zarah*, ch. 1 (regarding the Hananiah ben Teradion story on AZ 18a).

[22] *Mekhilta*, Ba-Hodesh, 6.

(1) The story of the binding of Isaac (Genesis 22) has been a source of perplexity throughout Jewish history. How could God "put Abraham to the test" by commanding him to prepare "your son, your favored one, whom you love, Isaac"[23] to be bound on an alter, presumably for child sacrifice in conformity with the norm throughout the ancient Near East? After all, the biblical God was supposed to be just, a trait on which Abraham himself relied in arguing for saving the city of Sodom,[24] and how can a just God demand the murder of the innocent Isaac? Moreover, after an extended period of infertility, God Himself had promised Abraham and Sarah that Isaac would be the beginning of a long line of descendants, and so how can God renege on his promise by demanding Isaac's sacrifice now? Furthermore, later God himself tells the Israelites in no uncertain terms that they are not to follow the practices of the worshipers of Moloch in sacrificing their children to the god,[25] and so how could He tell Abraham to do that very thing? Indeed, even though God originally demands that first-born sons be dedicated to Temple service, He later has parents substitute a payment to the priest in lieu of such service;[26] He certainly cannot be portrayed as demanding the very lives of our children!

Despite all these questions, because God declares in the biblical story that He sees Abraham's willingness to sacrifice his son as proof of his faith,[27] Jews in the Middle Ages often invoked this story to find meaning in their own acts of martyrdom. They reasoned that if God found Abraham worthy for merely being willing to sacrifice his son, how much more must God find medieval Jews worthy who actually did martyr themselves and their families for the sanctification of the Divine Name. Some even revised the story in the retelling, such that Abraham actually sacrifices his son, depending on the fact that in the biblical account Abraham came to the mountain with his servants and with Isaac but leaves only with his servants.[28] What happened to Isaac? Was he sacrificed after all? That

---

[23] Genesis 22:2.
[24] Genesis 18:23-25.
[25] Leviticus 18:21; 20:2-5; cf. 2 Kings 23:10; Jeremiah 7:31; 32:35; and, possibly, Ezekiel 36:18.
[26] Exodus 13:1; 22:28; Numbers 3:12.
[27] Genesis 22:12, 15-18.
[28] Genesis 22:19.

would make the Abraham story even more of a model for medieval Jews sacrificing themselves and their families rather than letting the Crusaders kill them in the name of Christ.[29]

(2) Medieval Jews similarly used the apocryphal story of an unnamed woman (but later called Hannah) and her seven sons.[30] In poignant terms, the sources depict how, one by one, the seven brothers voluntarily submitted to torture and death rather than obey the king's command to eat swine's flesh as part of a Greek rite, and then the mother, having encouraged them to keep true to their Jewish faith and having witnessed the martyrdom of all seven, herself refuses to participate in the pagan cult and dies a martyr's death. This compelling story of faith, depicted as taking place during the religious persecutions of Antiochus IV Epiphanes in the 167-166 B.C.E., undoubtedly served as a source for the law that emerged some four centuries later demanding death rather than participation in public idolatry. The story also served as a model for medieval and modern Jews who martyred themselves and their families rather than abandoning Judaism.

(3) Another famous story of Jewish martyrdom, but a more complex one, is the account by Josephus of the Zealots' martyrdom at Masada,[31] a story to which Ziering specifically refers as a possible justification for Herbert Bierhoff's killing of his daughter, Ellen.[32] Josephus records a

---

[29] On the later interpretations and uses of this story, see Shalom Spiegel, *The Last Trial: On the Legends and Lore of the Command to Abraham to Offer Isaac as a Sacrifice*, Judah Goldin, trans. (Philadelphia: Jewish Publication Society, 1967).

[30] 2 Maccabees, chs. 6 and 7; cf. 4 Maccabees 5:4ff and 8:3ff; B. *Gittin* 57b; *Lamentations* Rabbah 1:16, #50; Yalkut *Shimoni*, on Deuteronomy 26, #938 and on Lamentations #1029; *Peskita Rabbati* 43:180; *Seder Eliyahu Rabbah*, 30:151. In the early versions the woman is unnamed, but because of the influence of the line in Hannah's prayer that speaks of a mother of seven being forlorn (I Samuel 2:5), a Spanish revisor of the *Josippon* (ed. Constantinople, 1510, 4:19) called her Hannah, and later poets and storytellers used that name. See Gerson D. Cohen, "The Story of Hannah and Her Seven Sons in Hebrew Literature," in *Mordecai M. Kaplan Jubilee Volume* (New York: Jewish Theological Seminary, 1953), Hebrew section, pp. 109ff; and "Hannah and Her Seven Sons," *Encyclopedia Judaica* 7:1270-1272.

[31] Josephus, *Wars* 7:320ff.

[32] Sigi Ziering, *The Judgment of Herbert Bierhoff*, 81.

valiant speech by Eleazar ben Yair, commander of the Zealots at Masada from 66 until its fall in 73 C.E., in which he persuades his comrades, after the Romans breached Masada's walls, to kill themselves rather than let the Romans take them.

They then chose ten men by lot from among them to slay all the rest, every one of whom lay himself down by his wife and children on the ground and threw his arms about them as they offered their necks to the stroke of those who by lot executed that melancholy task. When these ten had, without fear, slain them all, they made the same rule of casting lots for themselves, that the one whose lot it was should first kill the other nine, and after all should kill himself...So these people died with this intention, that they would leave not so much as one soul among them all alive to be subject to the Romans...The dead were 960 in number...The Romans came within the palace, and so met with the multitude of the slain, but could take no pleasure in the fact, though this had been done to their enemies. Nor could they do other than wonder at the courage of their resolution and the immovable contempt of death that so great a number as they had shown....[33]

This martyrdom was not explicitly for religious reasons, for the Romans to this point had not made the Jews worship Roman gods or do anything to deny Judaism. Indeed, according to the famous talmudic story, just three years earlier Rabban Yohanan ben Zakkai, after being carried surreptitiously out of Jerusalem in a coffin, negotiated with the Romans to let him reestablish the Sanhedrin in Yavneh.[34] The story of Masada, like the entire war against the Romans, was instead political in nature, with the goal of reestablishing Jewish rule over Jews. Thus, if modern, secular Israelis look to the Maccabees for inspiration to fight oppressors, they like the Masada story even more because it models military action and even self-sacrifice not for religion but for political autonomy. Presumably, *if* the Zealots were warranted in killing themselves and their children to avoid national shame and slavery—a debatable question—Herbert Bierhoff was even more justified in killing Ellen lest she be killed or forcibly converted to Christianity.

---

[33] Josephus, *Wars* 7:9, 1.
[34] B. *Gittin* 56b.

(4) The Talmud also records a story of four hundred boys and girls who jumped into the sea to drown rather than submit to sodomy or rape:

It once happened that 400 boys and girls were abducted to be abused (Rashi's comment: the boys for sodomy and the girls for harems). When they realized why they were taken, they said, "If we drown in the sea, we will attain the life to come"...They all jumped and fell into the sea.[35]

The Talmud simply tells the story, without declaring the children's actions right or wrong. Furthermore, the story recalls what children did, and they may have understood Jewish law on the matter incorrectly; after all, Rabbi Hananyah ben Teradiyon refused to commit suicide. The twelfth-and-thirteenth-century Ashkenazi rabbis called the Tosafot (several of whom were Rashi's grandchildren), though, suggest two possible justifications for that suicide despite the contrary example of: (a) They were afraid of torture; (b) They would be forced to sin without even the option of choosing death instead. For the Tosafot, then, either of these reasons justifies taking one's own life as a permissible act of martyrdom when confronted with hostile Gentiles.[36]

(5) Yet another story of Jewish martyrdom is that of the Ten Martyrs who endured excruciating deaths at the hands of the Romans for the crime of teaching Torah. This story has become part of the liturgy of the Day of Atonement in the Musaf service (the *Eleh Ezkerah* poem by Eliezer

---

[35] B. *Gittin* 47b. The Talmud also contains the stories of the servant of Rabbi Judah, the President of the Sanhedrin, who killed himself when learning of his master's death (B. *Ketubbot* 103b), and of the pagan executioner who jumps into the flames killing Rabbi Hananiah ben Teradyon to join him in death and in the World to Come the rabbi promised him (B. *Avodah Zarah* 18a).

[36] The first reason, fear of torture, is not usually taken to justify suicide on the part of those who suffer medically or psychologically. Only one medieval source seems to justify that—the *Besamim Rosh*, attributed to Rabbenu Asher (1250-1327)—according to which a man who committed suicide because he could no longer tolerate the dire poverty and degradation of his life is permitted full burial rights. The more normative opinion is that what differentiates permissible martyrdom from prohibited suicide is a religious motive. For example, Maimonides says that even though Jewish law highly prizes life and health, a person who has an incurable illness may not violate the three cardinal sins (murder, incest, idolatry) in the name of trying to recover from it, for such an act is considered voluntary. If the goal is to avoid religious coercion by Gentiles, however, there is no statutory punishment. M.T. *Laws of the Foundations of the Torah* 5:4, 6.

Kallir), and it is the source for one of the religious dirges (*kinot*) recited on the fast of the Ninth of Av (Tisha B'Av), namely, *Arzeri Ha-levanon Adirei Ha-Torah*. Because of its inclusion in these liturgical places, the story of the Ten Martyrs is relatively well-known, even though it is a late medieval legend based, in part, on some talmudic accounts of the martyrdoms of a number of rabbis from the period of the war against the Romans in 66-70 until the Hadrianic persecutions after the Bar Kokhba Revolt of 132-135.[37] Whatever its origins, it is another story in the popular Jewish mind that would model and justify martyrdom for the faith.

(6) Another story that Ziering mentions[38] is that of the Jews in the Rhineland in the eleventh and twelfth centuries who killed their children and themselves before the Crusaders could do that.[39] Wherever possible, Jews tried to fight off their assailants at the gates of the city and even at the entrances to their houses, but when their efforts failed, they first killed their children in order to prevent their being captured and raised as Christians and then killed themselves to prevent their own torture and possible conversion. This regrettably became so common that some medieval Jewish prayer books include a benediction to be recited by Jews before killing themselves and their children. Graphic accounts of these events by Jewish survivors exist in several languages, and they tell a gruesome, but courageous, story. For example, an account by Solomon

---

[37] The number ten apparently was intended to correspond to the ten sons of Jacob who sold Joseph into slavery; cf. *Midrash Proverbs* to 1:13. The list of ten martyrs is first enumerated in *Leviticus Rabbah* 2:2, with no description of how they were put to death. The full story appears for the first time in *Heikhalot Rabbati*, composed in the circles of the mystics who studied Ezekiel's vision of the Heavenly Chariot (the "*Ba'alei Merkavah*"). Some of the deaths included in the story are described in the Talmud, including Rabbi Hananyah ben Teradyon (B. *Avodah Zarah* 17b-18a); Rabbi Akiba (B. *Menahot* 29b), and Rabbi Judah ben Bava (B. *Sanhedrin* 14a). See "The Ten Martyrs," *Encyclopedia Judaica* 15:1006-1008.

[38] Ziering, *The Judgment of Herbert Bierhoff*, 82.

[39] Tragic stories also emerge in the fourteenth and fifteenth centuries of Spanish Jews who, in the face of the Inquisition, chose to go underground with their faith (as marranos, Spanish for "pigs," or, in Hebrew, *anusim*, those forced [to convert]), to move away, or to die for the sake of Judaism. As terrible as that choice was, though, they did have a choice, unlike their Rhineland cousins, and we do not hear of their sacrificing their children except when they themselves chose to die rather than leave or convert.

bar Samson in approximately 1140 of the 1,100 people slaughtered by the Crusaders in Mayence on May 27, 1096, describes the valiant efforts of the Jewish community to defend themselves, although outnumbered by a ratio of twelve to one, and then, in gory detail, their sacrifice of their children and themselves. The author then includes this paragraph:

> Thus were the precious children of Zion, the Jews of Mayence, tried with ten trials like Abraham, our father, and like Hananiah, Mishael, and Azariah [who were thrown into a fiery furnace, Daniel 3:21]. They tied their sons as Abraham tied Isaac, his son, and they received upon themselves with a willing soul the yoke of the fear of God, the King of Kings, the Holy One, blessed be He, rather than deny and exchange the religion of our King for [Isaiah 14:19] "an abhorred offshoot" [Jesus]... The ears of him who hears these things will tingle, for who has ever heard anything like this? Inquire now and look about: Was there every such an abundant sacrifice as this since the days of the primeval Adam? Were there ever eleven hundred offerings on one day, each one of them like the sacrifice of Isaac, son of Abraham?[40]

Note the sheer horror the author still has in recalling the events 44 years later, and note that he compares it to the "sacrifice" of Isaac, as if Isaac had actually been killed by Abraham. In other communities, Jews chose suicide rather than allow Christians to torture them and extract "confessions" of killing Christians for their blood to be used on Passover (the blood libels) or of desecrating the Christian Host, or of causing the Black Plague, for then there was the additional motivation of depriving Christians of false confessions to these calumnies against the Jews.

(7) Finally, stories seemingly without number from the Holocaust add to this gruesome list of Jewish martyrs. Many of the Jews of Berlin committed suicide, but Rabbi Ephraim Oshry, rabbi of the Kovno ghetto,

---

[40] "The Crusaders in Mayence, May 27, 1096," in *The Jew in the Medieval World: A Source Book*, Jacob R. Marcus, ed. (New York: Union of American Hebrew Congregations, 1938; New York: Harper and Row, 1965), 117-118.

takes pride in the fact that only three members of his community took their own lives, a fact which he sees as a graphic demonstration of the remarkable depth of faith of his contemporary Jews.[41] Leib Garfunkel, a member of the Council of Elders, confirms that figure until the last week of the existence of the ghetto:

> ....there were hardly any suicides. From any rational point of view there were more than enough reasons to warrant putting an end to one's afflictions and tortures. Yet it is worthy of note that from the time of the outbreak of the war between the Soviet Union and Germany through the period of the establishment of the ghetto—except for the very last days—there were no more than two or three suicides of Jews. Only in the last week, when it became known for certain that the ghetto and its labor camps were to be destroyed and the remaining Jews transported to Germany—there almost certainly to be slaughtered—only then did the number of suicides in the ghetto increase. But even in that week, the number was relatively small.[42]

In his Warsaw diary, Chaim Kaplan attempts to explain this phenomenon of the low rate of suicide among the Jews of Eastern Europe as a manifestation of "a certain invisible power embedded in us, and it is this secret which keeps us alive and preserves us in spite of all the laws of nature." He speaks of German and Austrian Jewry, by contrast, who committed suicide by the thousands, with whole families "voluntarily" taking their own lives due to fear. He maintains that the Polish Jewish community took another path because of its stronger roots in Jewish tradition:

> Not so with the beaten-down, shamed, broken Jews of Poland. They love life, and they do not wish to disappear

---

[41] Irving J. Rosenbaum, *The Holocaust and Halakhah* (New York: Ktav, 1976), p. 39. Also in Rabbi Ephraim Oshry, *Responsa from the Holocaust*, Y. Leiman, trans. from Oshry's *She'elot u'Teshuvot Mi-Ma'amakim [Questions and Answers from the Depths]* (New York: Judaica Press, 1983), 34-35.
[42] Rosenbaum, *ibid.*, 39-40.

from the earth before their time. The fact that we have
hardly any suicides is worthy of special emphasis. Say
what you wish, this will of ours to live in the midst of
terrible calamity is the outward manifestation of a certain
hidden power...which is rooted in our eternal tradition
that command us to live.[43]

There is clearly more than a little triumphalism here in his expressions
of pride in his own Polish community in contrast to the more assimilated
Jewish communities of Germany and Austria. One even detects a certain
meanness in that pride. Still, he bespeaks a strong Jewish tradition to avoid
suicide and to cling to life. The question, though, is that of Sigi Ziering's
play: Does that demand to choose life extend even to cases like the Holocaust,
where humiliation, torture, and ultimately death are all but certain? Even if
one can find Jewish warrant for living to one's natural end despite anything
other human beings may do to you, can one also find Jewish justification
for killing yourself and your children under the conditions of the Holocaust?
Indeed, was Sigi Ziering motivated to write his play by the example of the
German Jews who did just that?

The Ultimate Question: The Judgment of Herbert Bierhoff

First, as one who did not live through the Holocaust (I was born in
the United States in 1943), I feel a distinct lack of moral standing to
judge what people faced with those horrible choices did. As Hillel said,
"Do not judge your fellow human being until you stand in his place."[44]
Thus it is important that in Ziering's play, it is survivors of the Holocaust
that are carrying on the dialogue, for if anyone has such standing, they do.

If asked what the Jewish tradition would say about the matter, though,
the sources that I described above would push people strongly to avoid
suicide, and certainly those who did so have amply warrant within the
tradition for their steadfastness and bravery. On the other hand, though,
some sources within the tradition would deal sympathetically with people
who committed suicide and even with those who killed others under

[43] *Ibid.*, 40.
[44] M. *Avot (Ethics of the Fathers)* 2:5.

certain circumstances. Exactly how to define the limits of those situations, however, is hard, for we are never quite sure whether a given case is to be a model for everyone or whether a given law is to be applied across the board or only more narrowly. So, for example, Rabbi Oshry of the Kovno ghetto in the end permitted someone who had committed suicide to have full burial rights despite the example of Rabbi Hananyah ben Teradiyon, who refused to commit suicide under duress, because, Rabbi Oshry ruled, Rabbi Hananyah was especially pious and therefore not a standard for ordinary Jews.[45]

In analyzing the specific case presented in the play, I have some of the same questions that several of the characters raise. Specifically, if Herbert Bierhoff was so convinced of the murderous intentions of the Nazis, why did he not also commit suicide? The cynical way of putting that is this: Why did he deny his child the chance to survive, however slight it was, without denying himself that same chance? In the end, as Shimon says, some children did in fact survive, even though their number was small and their suffering great.

Although we never hear about Herbert Bierhoff's motivations for killing Ellen in the play, several possible ones come immediately to mind. He may, as Kurt suggests,[46] have acted out of love and pity for Ellen, killing her to help her avoid what he knew would be, at best, excruciating pain. Most Jewish sources do not permit suicide—let alone, murder—for reasons of avoiding pain; instead they advocate continuing to live life while doing what one can to quell the pain. Still, Ellen was five years old, and could Herbert have reasonably expected her to know how to do that? Clearly not! A teenager, maybe, or even a child of ten or twelve, but not a five-year-old.

Another way to read his motives is more in line with established Jewish law: Even though the Nazis were not at all interested in converting Jews to Christianity, perhaps Herbert feared that they would force her to deny her Jewish faith before they tortured and killed her. Or, along the same lines, perhaps he feared that a sympathetic Christian family would find her before the Nazis did and raise her as a Christian. Under such circumstances, talmudic law specifically permits giving up your own life,

---

[45] Rosenbaum, *The Holocaust and Halakhah*, 39.
[46] Ziering, *The Judgment of Herbert Bierhoff*, 78.

but it does not permit taking the lives of your children. Still, the examples of the Jews of the Rhineland, who murdered their children before committing suicide, might stand as a model for Herbert's case, for later rabbis justified what the Rhenish Jews did.

But then again, the Jews of the Rhineland also took their own lives; why did Herbert fail to do that? Was it, as Esther suggests, that he believed suicide to be prohibited by God and was therefore to take whatever suffering the Nazis imposed on him but could not stand by to see his daughter endure the same? Or was it, as David suggests, that he wanted to be punished for having killed his daughter, knowing that the Nazis would be only too happy to oblige?[47]

If Herbert had asked me as a rabbi at the time what to do, I probably, as a representative of the Jewish tradition, would have advised him not to kill her and to do what he could to save whomever he could. After all, Jewish law does value life above almost everything else, and Herbert could not have known that she would be among the many who died rather than the few who lived. (In medical circumstances, some have argued on this basis that no withdrawal of life support systems is legitimate, for every moment of life is sacred. I have not taken that position; I would allow even the withdrawal of artificial nutrition and hydration from a dying patient for whom there is no reasonable hope for recovery in the context of current medical practice. In those circumstances, though, it is the underlying disease that is taking the person's life, and medical experience affords us some assurance of the chances of people in such circumstances to live or die; here we are talking about the vagaries of what will happen to Ellen and what the human beings who encounter her will choose to do, and there, despite the Nazis' known murderous intentions, her future is more doubtful, as indicated by the children who survived the Holocaust.)

At the same time, if Herbert pressed me with worries about the sheer pain Ellen would suffer, and if he said that he himself could not endure the thought of letting her be subjected to such pain, I would probably fall silent. I could not, in all good conscience, assure him that the Jewish tradition condoned the murder of his child. At the same time, knowing what Jews knew about the Nazis in the fall of 1943, I could not myself know whether this situation now confronting us under the Nazis was *sui*

---

[47] *Ibid.*, 78.

generis, such that none of the normal rules applied. I could also empathize with his pain and with his passion to protect his daughter from pain. Still, I would not know whether that constituted grounds for murdering her.

And so, in the end, we are faced with clear instructions from the tradition—"You shall not murder"—and yet circumstances that raise serious questions about whether that clear command should be straightforwardly applied. The medieval Rhineland communities feared not only for their lives, but also that they or their children would be forcibly converted to Christianity. But that was not part of the Nazi agenda. Thus, I tend to agree with Rabbi Oshry when he says that if all the Jews were to kill themselves and their children in the face of the Nazi terror, that would in itself be a victory for the Nazis, for it would not only fulfill the wish of the murderers to extinguish the Jews, but it would also mark the Jews' own abandonment of faith in Judaism and hope for God's salvation to "rescue them from the impure and cursed hands of the Nazis."[48] Still, while I can say what I think the Jewish tradition would instruct Herbert to do, I cannot say with certainty—especially after the fact—that what he did was wrong. And so I think of him and his terrible choice with compassion and respect.

---

[48] Rosenbaum, *The Holocaust and Halakhah,* 39.

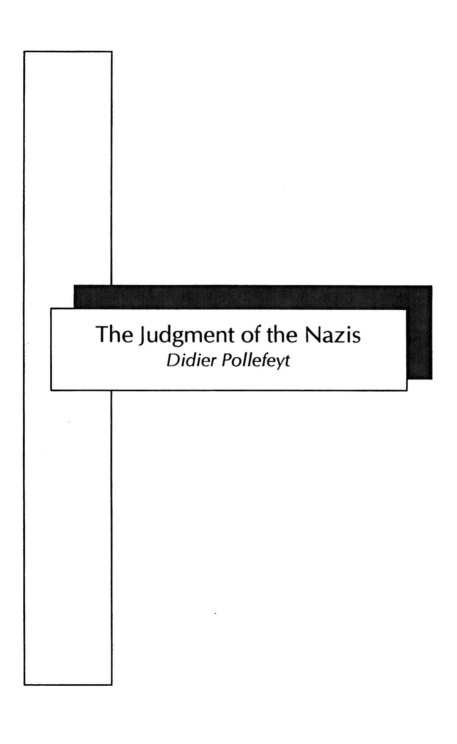

The Judgment of the Nazis
Didier Pollefeyt

From a moral perspective, the story of Herbert Bierhoff is a *casus perplexus*: it not only shocks, but also paralyzes our moral capacity. Post *Shoah* ethics has taught us an unconditional respect for every human life, since Auschwitz was a most violent attack on the basis of every ethics: "Thou shall not kill." And now, we are confronted with a Jewish father killing his own daughter to save her from a brutal death in the hands of the Nazis.

In the light of this moral drama, some escape routes become very tempting. I will distinguish three: 1. moral condemnation, 2. insiderism and 3. ethisation. I will criticize all three of these moral solutions. They are, in my view, pitfalls in our search for an adequate moral understanding of this tragic moment in the history of the *Shoah*.

Defenders of the moral principle of the "sanctity" of human life will strongly condemn the action of Herbert Bierhoff, since, for them, human life has absolute and sacred value.[1] In this perspective, killing is always an (intrinsic) evil act, even if it is done with good intentions to avoid a greater evil. Sometimes defenders of the sanctity-of-life principle will even refer to the *Shoah* as a warning against the use of "mercy killing," since this idea was exploited by the Nazis to legitimize their genocide. It is not surprising that in the current euthanasia debate, the Holocaust is often referred to by the opponents of

---

[1] Paul M. Quay, "The Sacredness of the Human Person: Cessation of Treatment" in *Linacre Quarterly* 59 (1992), 77-79.

euthanasia as a strong argument in favor of their position.[2] Life is an absolute good and every effort that questions this in the name of another (particular) good is unacceptable, because this particular good is seen as subjective, manipulatable and contingent. The Bierhoff case can be interpreted in that light: Bierhoff is morally wrong, and should be condemned, because he violated the deontological rule: "you shall (never) kill."

In our view, the story of Bierhoff reveals precisely the limits of this very moralistic approach. To condemn Bierhoff massively from a moral point of view for killing his daughter would be very cruel and unfair, since it is not taking into account the intentions and the context of his action, but only looks to the material act of killing as such. The extreme circumstances of Nazi persecution reveals that there are situations where the notion of the sanctity of life as such in its absolute form becomes untenable and even inhuman.

In the story told by Ziering, it is very startling that after the killing of his daughter, Bierhoff himself is executed by the Nazis because in their judgment he is a "child murderer" (p. 23). "The *Fuehrer* is right: you Jews are nothing but an inferior race without any morals" (p. 23). The killing of Bierhoff's daughter is even used by the Nazis to legitimize the next day's *Aktion* "to prevent further killings of innocent children by these damned Jews." The Nazis accuse Bierhoff of the murder of his daughter. They execute Bierhoff for his lack of morality. People who condemn Bierhoff, risk in fact to end up in the same camp as the Nazis, when they only look to the material act of killing itself, and make in that way of morality a cold monster. Nazism cannot only be interpreted as an extreme example of ethical relativism (as hard opponents of euthanasia do), but can also be understood as an extreme example of ethical absolutism (calling the Jew e.g. an absolute evil in itself).[3]

In confrontation with this position of moral condemnation, the question becomes: "Is every killing a murder?" Can killing not have many moral

---

[2] Cynthia B. Cohen, "Quality of Life and the Analogy with the Nazis" in James J. Walter & Thomas A. Shannon (eds.), *Quality of Life: The New Medical Dilemma* (New York: Paulist Press, 1990), 61-77.

[3] Didier Pollefeyt, "The Kafkaesque World of the Holocaust. Paradigmatic Shifts in the Interpretation of the Holocaust" in J.K. Roth (ed.), *Ethics After the Holocaust. Perspectives, Critiques and Responses* (Paragon Books on the Holocaust) (St. Paul: Paragon House, 1999), 210-242.

meanings? We can make an analogy with stealing. Is stealing always wrong? In the Bierhoff story, we read an interesting definition of "organizing" in the camps: "like stealing, but God doesn't punish you for organizing" [because it is stealing from the Nazis in a camp to survive the Nazi evil]. In the same way, should we not look to the context and the intentions to evaluate from a moral perspective Bierhoff's material act of killing?

This brings us to two other tempting approaches of the Bierhoff case. Looking to the context can bring us to insiderism (second approach), looking to the intentions can result in ethisation (third approach).

"Insiderism"[4] is the affirmation of an unbridgeable rupture of knowledge and communication between insiders (victims) and outsiders (non-victims). Because outsiders lack some formal conditions of knowledge, they have problems or are even unable to come to real empathy or moral understanding concerning life in the concentration camps or the ghettos. It is clear that the author of *The Judgment of Herbert Bierhoff* is rather in favor of insiderism as an important tool to deal with the Bierhoff case. Some of the characters in the play, especially Shimon and Kurt, often speak of an absolute monopoly of knowledge of the insider. They stress that the "circumstances surrounding the case are so far beyond comprehension" and may well be "beyond imagination" (p. 71) of anyone except the survivors. And there are good reasons for that line of argumentation. The experience of the ghettos and camps is so radical and so deviant that the suggestion of monopoly of many insiders at first glance doesn't need any further justification. Indeed, the more extreme the experience, the greater the distance between the world of the insider and the outsider, and the more "insiderism" becomes acceptable. The presuppositions of the ghetto and camp experience had so little common ground with the presuppositions of life outside the ghettos and camps, that most of the prisoners did not have convenient tools to express their ghetto or camp experience to themselves and to others. Ziering writes: "There is no continuity, no transition: it is an Either/Or state of mind" (p. 81). An extreme outcome of this insideristic position is the "invention of the devil" (p. 72) to

---

[4] Didier Pollefeyt, "Insiderism": Cornerstone or Stumbling Block for Relations between Survivors and Scholars of the Holocaust?" in S. Leder and M. Teichman (eds.), *The Burden of History: Post Holocaust Generations in Dialogue* (Selected Papers from the 29th Annual International Scholars' Conference on the Holocaust and the Churches, March 6-9, 1999, Nassau Community College, Garden City, New York) (Merion: Westfield Press International, 2000), 117-128.

deal with the problems of the *Shoah*, since the event is "totally inconsistent and unexplainable within the context of religion or human experience" (p. 72).

Insiderism and diabolization are understandable, extreme ways of dealing with the Holocaust. Nevertheless, these phenomena are very problematic because by refusing any parallel with common human experience, they make the *Shoah* in a paradoxical way irrelevant from a moral point of view. Insiderism also contains other risks. Insiders often refer to their personal experience and knowledge to reject radically the understanding and judging of outsiders. And, of course, experience produces unique insight, especially such radical experiences, but experience doesn't automatically guarantee correct insight. On the contrary, experience can also limit, distort and even obstruct insight. If insiderism would be a correct position, Holocaust scholarship would become impossible in principle. This is not only true for Holocaust Studies, but for all human sciences. *In extremis*, only black, female, homosexual, Catholic, Jewish, etc., scholars could then do significant research about blacks, women, homosexuals, Catholics, Jews, etc. Insiderism conducts to a "balkanization" of human sciences. It makes historiography and moral reflection on the *Shoah* senseless. It becomes even irrelevant to ask Shimon's question: "How would you have acted in Bierhoff's place?" (p. 75).

So the Holocaust scholar, as an outsider, is put in confrontation with this case, in a paradoxical position: He is asked to reflect upon an event during the Holocaust, but at the same time, by insiderism, he is declared to be structurally incompetent to do that. A consequence of this position is that the Holocaust can finally hold no moral message for human beings today, since the event is the work of the devil living in another world. And the Holocaust risks to die together with the last survivor. The *Shoah* is only relevant to our world when it is the work of human beings and when there is at least some kind of continuity between then and now, here and there. And there was continuity: The *Shoah* was the work of men living in the center of modern and Christian Europe.

A third and last strategy (next to moral condemnation and insiderism) to deal with the Bierhoff case is to concentrate (exclusively) on the (good) intentions of Herbert Bierhoff. I call this strategy the "ethisation": to understand the act of Bierhoff (exclusively) in the light of the ethical values he wants to realize. It is very clear to the reader of the story that Bierhoff acted out of care and love for his daughter. I do not agree that Herbert Bierhoff did "act on his own, independent of any commandments or belief in God," as Esther argues. I think he acted *in the name of* the commandment of love or in God's name.

Bierhoff chose a mercy killing for his beloved daughter, in order to avoid an infinitely more brutal killing by the SS. In the opinion of the character David, the killing was an act of "pure love" (p. 76). We are here at the opposite of the first position: The killing is not pure evil, but a good, perhaps a pure good.

Even if the act of killing can be inspired by good intentions, we can nevertheless not deny that in some way the act itself is contaminated with evil too. In and by itself, as a material act, killing is an evil. From an ethical perspective, one never kills for pleasure. Killing itself can never be a moral good. But sometimes, we can only realize something good, by accepting also a (particular) evil. It is in this kind of complex and dramatic situation that Bierhoff was involved. He has chosen to kill his daughter, not because this is a good as such, but to avoid a greater evil. Even if no one uses the argument in the story, thanks to her father, Ellen could die in the warmth of her house and her bed, surrounded by the love of her parents. Herbert Bierhoff's love was pure, but the context was not, neither were the consequences of his actions. The whole case reveals especially the complexity, even the inseparability of good and evil. By doing something good, we sometimes give evil a helping hand. We can have good intentions and evil consequences, or a good consequence and an evil consequence, or a less evil consequence and a greater good consequence.

One has not only to look to the intentions and the circumstances, but also to the material act itself, as well as to the consequences of a moral act: consequences on the short and the long term, on the individual and the collective level, direct and indirect consequences, predictable and unpredictable consequences. The killing of Bierhoff's daughter had terrible (for him mostly unpredictable) consequences, not only for his own daughter and for his own life, but also for the other Jewish children in the ghetto. So, if he wanted it or not, Bierhoff became involved in evil (perhaps he was already involved by being a member of the Jewish Ghetto Police), even by doing a good. This is a well-known conclusion when studying the Holocaust from a moral perspective, as Hannah Arendt has taught us. In a paradoxical way, the Jews sometimes played into the hands of their oppressors, facilitated their task, and brought closer their own perdition, while guided in their actions by rationality and morality. But finally—a fact that Arendt mistakenly forgot—

the perpetrators, not the victims were responsible for these perverted circumstances.[5]

We have analyzed until now three classical and, at first glance, attractive approaches of the Bierhoff case:

1. A deontological approach that condemns the killing of Ellen morally on the basis of the rule "You shall not kill";

2. An Insideristic approach that refuses any moral condemnation, even every moral judgment on the basis of the extreme and even diabolical context in which Bierhoff had to act;

3. An intentionalistic approach that recognizes and praises the good intention of the actor.

All three of these approaches have been criticized: the first, because it refuses to take into consideration the context and the intentions of the act; the second because it makes the Holocaust finally morally irrelevant, and the third because it forgets to take into account the dramatic material act of killing itself, as much as the consequences of this action. But each of these approaches also reveals aspects to judge from a moral point of view Herbert Bierhoff's action. These three approaches need each other. To come to a moral evaluation, we have to look *at the same time* to: the material act itself, the context, the intention and the consequences of the action.

Killing in itself is never a good as such. The formal act of killing is always a (particular) evil, because even if life is not an absolute good, it is a basic good. Even if the killing of Ellen is (from the perspective of the intention) an act of "pure love," it still remains an act of killing of a human being, which can never be a good *an sich*. Killing is always problematic, because death is something that strikes us as a non- or anti-value. This is what is expressed in the deontological rule: "You shall not kill." So the Bierhoff case is not only an act of pure love, but also a very complex and ambivalent action, because the loving father becomes involved in evil by acting out of love: he realizes an anti-value, the death of his daughter. Of course, he had good reasons to kill his daughter, that is, to save her from a greater evil. The Bierhoff case confronts us with the ambiguity and the complexity of good and evil. Here, the context becomes very important. In his situation, Bierhoff is confronted with a moral

---

[5] Didier Pollefeyt, "Victims of Evil or Evil of Victims?" in H.J. Cargas (ed.), *Problems Unique to the Holocaust* (Lexington: The University Press of Kentucky, 1999), 67-82.

dilemma: He had to save two values, on the one side to give his daughter a "better death," on the other side to give her a last chance to survive. He couldn't save both values at the same time! Or, he had to choose between two incompatible non- and anti-values: to kill his daughter himself or to deliver his daughter to the violent murder by the Nazis.

Insiderism will argue that we have no right to judge in that context the decision Bierhoff made. I think, however, that we can understand and even judge Bierhoff's choice from a moral perspective. He made a sincere proportional weighing of pros and contras, values and non or anti-values at stake at that moment, in that context, and he decided that by killing his daughter, he could save more values and eliminate more non- or anti-values than by keeping her alive.

Not every killing is a murder in the same way as "organizing" is not the same as stealing. There can be proportionate reasons to kill. So killing is and remains an evil, never desirable as such, but there can be (and there are) sometimes proportional heavier moral reasons to kill, because there are other (greater) goods that must be saved (by killing). And these kinds of proportional moral reasoning are not typical for situations of war and genocide, but can also emerge in daily life. Of course, in the Bierhoff case, the moral dilemma is extremely sharp, due to the exceptional circumstances, but the difference between normal life and ghetto and camp life is a matter of degree, not a matter of radical difference (insiderism).

If we accept this approach, then we have to ask the question if and to what extent Bierhoff did (not) make the correct weighing of conflicting values and non- or anti-values, goods and evils. To begin with, no one will question the fact that Bierhoff did this weighing based on a good intention. In this sense, we can agree that the killing of his daughter was an act of "pure love." But a good intention does not automatically end up in a good moral action. The central question is: In this context, which values and non- and anti-values were at stake? Bierhoff had to compare the chance for a longer life for his daughter with the risk of her terrible death. One can argue that he was not completely certain that Ellen would be transported and killed the next day(s) and that her death was so imminent. Perhaps Bierhoff projected the fears about his own destiny on the future of his daughter? But on this point, Ziering's story is very clear: As a result of his somewhat privileged position, Bierhoff "*knew beyond doubt* the fate awaiting his beloved daughter in the next morning's Action" [my italics] (p. 76). Moreover, we can be almost sure that

Bierhoff had evaluated all other possible alternatives, to save the values and to evade the anti-values, but that none of these were realistic in that context. Of course, one could object by arguing that perhaps the next day the ghetto would have been liberated by the Allies, or that suddenly one of the perpetrators would have saved Bierhoff's family, or that he could have escaped the ghetto by a secret exit, etc. But given the context, these were not realistic scenarios, as history proved later on. Another counter argument that can be raised is perhaps Ellen could have enjoyed that last, extra day; again met one other time her friend Shimon, and enjoyed another (final) orange; or been with her parents until the last moments in the camps. As Ziering writes: "The will to live one more day or hour in this hell, to eat the next lousy meal, increased almost in direct proportion to the hardships encountered" (p. 77). But all these small values seem not to be strong enough to counterbalance the non- and anti-value of a very close, certain and brutal death in the hands of the enemy. In ethics, we should learn that "at the end of the road" (p. 78) more important than adding days to life, is to add life to our days. "Tomorrow, you are going on a trip where you'll have many oranges" (p. 20), Bierhoff tells to his daughter in a very moving way. In this context, the quality of Ellen's dying seems to be a very important value, even if no character in the story seems really to stress this. Finally, Ellen dies in her own sleeping room. Perhaps, it would have been humanly stronger if Bierhoff had involved his wife, the mother of Ellen, in his decision, as well as in the farewell scene. He has chosen not to do so, probably to save his wife from this terrible decision and from the dramatic separation and death of her child.

A last, difficult question to be asked is did Bierhoff sufficiently take into account the consequences of his act? Not only is his act misused by the Nazis to legitimate the killing of the other children, but also Bierhoff, himself, loses every chance to survive the war, since he is killed on the spot. This killing is a clear example of murder. The price he, himself, had to pay for the merciful death of his daughter is extremely high, perhaps too high. Of course, he could not anticipate all these consequences. It was not Bierhoff who was responsible for these consequences, but the perpetrators themselves. The Nazis violated the moral premises that human beings use to organize their life, and this fact shifts the guilt and responsibility of the cruelties from the victims to the criminals. The story is therefore a "judgment of the Nazis" (title of this essay), not a "judgment of Herbert Bierhoff" (title of Ziering's play). It must be emphasized that the value of something done by a human being does not only depend on the person who acts, but also on the humanity of the world in which this action is done. Insiderism makes that very clear. Nevertheless, the Bierhoff story illustrates that even in these extreme circumstances, ethical choices remained possible. Bierhoff could not choose the "pure good" any longer, but in his situation he was still able to choose between more evil or less evil. And he did. So he resisted the Nazi logic, not in a heroic act, but in a very dramatic way. One can question the argumentation at the basis of his decision, and the values that he gave the strongest weight, but one can certainly not call him a murderer.

In a context of extreme inhumanity, passing judgment becomes very difficult. An act can never be called good or bad in itself; this means that one must bear in mind the situation in which the subject finds himself at a certain moment and place, and the different values that are at stake then. The "true" identity of man will not reveal itself in such extreme circumstances, because man is not created for such situations. The greatest difference between Bierhoff and ourselves is not that he is a killer, and we are not, but that we have been saved from such tragic choices and he was not.

How can we look finally to the quest of Ruth to find competent judges who could declare that Herbert Bierhoff was merciful and right in giving Ellen the deadly pill? And how can that question be answered? As a Jew, Ruth is, for sure, educated with the Ten Commandments. She knows the fifth commandment: "Thou shall not kill." She feels that killing is always a non- and anti-value: a particular evil. She experiences that by the killing of his daughter, in some way Herbert Bierhoff had been contaminated by Nazi evil. In his resistance to Nazi evil, he became a collaborator of Nazi evil. Even if she knows that Bierhoff acted out of love for their daughter, she understands that evil is as a shadow inseparably following the good intention of her husband. She sees the complexity of good and evil, and she is overwhelmed by, and afraid of, moral condemnation. Insiderism is an understandable reaction here. It is a kind of mechanism of defense: "You have no right to judge, because you don't know the context from within." In a moral analysis that takes the context really into account, insiderism looses its necessity. And that is precisely the task of a judge!

Ruth's question can be seen as a critique on the insideristic position. She believes in the possibility to find a competent judge, and that's an extremely forceful position. By accepting the verdict of a judge, she implicitly also accepts the possibility that Herbert Bierhoff did morally wrong. Mostly, insiderism implies a radical separation between victim and perpetrator. A victim can do no evil, and a perpetrator can do no good! Accepting the judgment of a competent judge implies accepting at least the possibility that also the victim *can* do evil. Nevertheless, Ruth is prepared to take that risk. But she is convinced that her husband made the right decision, that he has made the correct proportional balancing between the different values and non- and anti-values at stake inspired by a fundamental good intention. And I believe every judge can see that she is right in her conviction and that guilt is to be directed towards the creators of that dramatic context: Nazism and the Nazis who manipulated and perverted the ethical context of Herbert Bierhoff and so many others. So Ruth is finally not only asking for the "judgment of Herbert Bierhoff," but in the first place for the "judgment of Nazism" itself.

But who can be this judge? Who can free Bierhoff, or the memory of Bierhoff, from guilt and responsibility for the death of his daughter? Ellen is no longer there to free her father. Can someone else do it in her place? In a religious (Judeo-Christian) context, God can. But also in this world, it must be possible, even if God does not exist. I think of people who represent more than themselves. In the first place, survivors—but not only survivors. It is a universal phenomenon that people are forever searching for someone who represents more than him/herself.[6] One can think of judges, and also of rabbis, imams, priests, etc. These independent secular and religious personalities can be adequate mediators and go-betweens, if they are open to all people and inspired by human rights (secular) and/or ecumenism (religious). They stand in secular and religious traditions and in communities in which good and evil are preserved, and in which people can call each other to justice and forgiveness. Such people can free Herbert Bierhoff from guilt and responsibility. This need not necessarily happen in a spectacular television show; it can happen in the smallest synagogue, in the most modest community, in any place in the world where the victims of the Holocaust are remembered. And it can happen with a sober symbolic act, because everywhere and anytime people can experience what goodness means, even under the rule of the most extreme evil. They can understand that Bierhoff did not collaborate with Nazi evil, but resisted it, or at least, tried to.

---

[6] A. Lascaris, *"Kan God vergeven als het slachtoffer niet vergeeft?"* in *Tijdschrift voor theologie* 39 (1999), 48-68.

Dream and Nightmare: Judging Herbert Bierhoff and Ourselves

Jonathan Freund

Dream and Nightmare

Jacob awoke from his sleep
and said: "Surely God is in this place,
and I did not know it!"
-Genesis 28:16

"God sent me...to do what?"
-Shimon, *The Judgment of Herbert Bierhoff*

As the child of a survivor and as father of a girl the same age as Ellen, Sigi Ziering's *The Judgment of Herbert Bierhoff* seizes me even as I recoil from it. Although I can never truly comprehend the horrific nature of the choice Herbert faced, his action shatters my faith and repels me. At the same time, I have compassion for him, and question how I would respond if I were in his place. That paradox risks causing moral paralysis, and it is therefore tempting to take refuge in the confidence, the faith and belief, that I personally will never face such a choice.

Yet that is to retreat from the Holocaust entirely, which is morally unacceptable. We so want to view the Holocaust on its monolithic scale, almost as if we find relief in its enormity, its impenetrability. Too often we forget that the entire Holocaust, every horrific or honorable act, occurred through the daily acts of ordinary men and women. The character Shimon speaks of our need to explain evil—and thus the *Shoah* itself—

as "strange and abnormal," of our "inability to acknowledge the capacity for evil in our fellow human beings." The *Shoah* may be the great dark forest of humanity; yet we must examine each individual tree if we are to find our way through it. The six million were killed one at a time; those that survived were spared one at a time. So I cannot turn away from the horror of Herbert Bierhoff's life—or from Ellen Bierhoff's death. I cannot because Sigi Ziering will not permit it.

However, neither do I know what my task is in response to the Holocaust. As Shimon, the driving force of the play and the audience-surrogate, asks on page 26: "God sent me...to do what?" The ellipse is crucial: It is the weighty silence of a question that arises only *after* we start to answer it. It is the question for all of us who live with the effects of the *Shoah* rather than memories of it: What does God ask us to *do* in response?

More specifically in this case, what does God ask us to do in response to a father who kills his daughter to save her from the Holocaust? Make no mistake, God does ask us to respond, if only because God *always* demands a response, to any and all events. It is not possible to isolate the Holocaust as an event outside of history. That, too, is to retreat from it— not just the facts of the Holocaust, but the implications of it.

As always, we must begin by listening to the victims. That means listening not just to the many survivors in Sigi Ziering's play, it means listening to the primary victim, Ellen Bierhoff.

Ellen—the child who makes a friend of a mouse, the child who does not understand math but who dreams of horses jumping to the clouds, who bites an orange through its bitter skin—is humanity existing in an inhumane world.

Even in the Riga Ghetto, her dreams are both pure and true. For Ellen, as for most children, there is no boundary between dream world and reality. It is as if she has no need of God. Her father, on the other hand, can only think of God: "God could make horses jump to the clouds if He wanted to," he tells Ellen. "*If He wanted to.*" That sounds as if Herbert is apologizing for, and at the same time accusing, an absent or unwilling God.

Still, he attempts to reassure Ellen with a bedtime fairy tale about how she will be going on a trip "to God" (p. 20). Certainly a man who is convinced his daughter will die tomorrow has abandoned faith in God and miracles, understandably so for a man who has seen too much of the

Godless world of the Riga Ghetto, and knows too much of what fate lies outside its walls. His very "certainty" about her future suffering, which compels him to take her life, would appear to deny the very existence of God. Instilling that very certainty is one of the Nazis greatest acts of inhumanity, one that makes the gross and horrifying deeds possible.

I find it curious that immediately after bidding goodbye to his daughter, Herbert misstates Ellen's dream to Ruth: "She told me a dream she had about going to heaven." Ellen said nothing about heaven, just as she says nothing about God. It is only adults who need heaven and God. Ellen's dreams are of flying horses, and walking in the clouds with her friends. Perhaps her father could not bear to see that harmony of reality and fantasy destroyed: He was not only protecting Ellen from physical agony but was unintentionally—one might even say, by the grace of God —saving childhood innocence itself.

That may sound too pat, unless we consider the *Shoah* as in part the utter negation of childhood, of innocence and dreams. It is no accident that the Nazis, indeed all totalitarian tyrants, begin by poisoning the minds of children, all children both ally or enemy.

My father occasionally spoke about suffering recurrent nightmares of his Berlin childhood: the sounds of *Kristallnacht*; being pelted with stones by *Wehrmacht* soldiers; forced to watch his school burned to the ground; and smaller but equally wrenching acts, such as losing his family's beloved German-Catholic nanny as a consequence of the Nuremberg Laws. Those events do not have the horrific force of an Auschwitz, or a Riga, but they still caused irreparable psychological damage. That damage —the murder of a childhood—is also a legacy of the Holocaust, one shared by every survivor still with us today.

Of course, even with that damage, my father survived, had an adult life, and became a parent himself. Ellen Bierhoff did not. Her fate was sealed by the Nazis, not by her father. He was saving her from the terror she was sure to know if she awoke the next morning.

Herbert feels that torment instead, as he spends the remaining hours of his life futilely digging his child's grave with a spoon in the unyielding Riga dirt. That is punishment enough for any man.

If only we could leave the story there. If only we could, like Esther in the play, "believe in the God who brought us out of Egypt and gave us the Torah at Sinai," without sharing her refusal to "believe the same God would have abandoned us during the Shoah" (p. 74). Why is it so unthinkable that God could do, and be, both?

Her statement also begs the question: *Did* God abandon Jews during *Shoah?* Ultimately, the Jews did survive, and in America and Israel, at least, we thrive as never before in our history. Perhaps then God was with the Jews all along. I say that fully aware of how abhorrent the idea may be to anyone who endured a camp or a ghetto, but as I noted earlier the Holocaust came about through the daily acts of men and women, not God. Many a survivor also credits his or her deliverance from those acts to a "miracle." Can we understand the actions of righteous gentiles as anything other than hearing and obeying the still small voice of the divine?

We should also remind Esther that God did not provide the miracles that delivered the Jews from Egypt until they had suffered 400 years of slavery, with all its degradation and death—and the organized mass murder of children, thrown to the crocodiles in the Nile.

Esther, apparently unintentionally, acknowledges that paradox herself, when she earlier declares: "...not believing after the Shoah is as irrational as believing" (p. 73). Belief itself—and faith and hope—are irrational, crazy, foolish. The act of a child, a child who believes in flying horses. The same child whom Herbert seeks to protect by killing her. Esther's paradox is our paradox, inherent in the human condition, and in our relationship with God.

In a similar manner, Shimon's nightmare is our nightmare: "I see myself as Herbert Bierhoff and wonder what I would have done in his place" (p. 74). That is why we must judge: because one day we may find ourselves in Herbert's place. On that day, when the knock on the door comes, there will be no symposium, no time for wrestling with questions. The knock comes as dinner waits on the table or as a child sleeps. In the end, what purpose does moral judgment serve if not to prepare ourselves for that moment?

We take as an act of philosophical comfort and religious faith that to ask the question, to wrestle with it, is more important than finding an answer. Yet Ziering's play implies questions we may not even want to wrestle with: If we understand, maybe even forgive Herbert for killing his own daughter to spare her, as a kind of rescuer—how would we feel if he poisoned other children, to spare them as well?

And would that not be a *more* heroic and honorable act?

Yes, Herbert "saves" his daughter by allowing her to die peacefully, dreaming, but at dawn hundreds if not thousands of other children will go screaming in terror and pain, all too conscious.

Certainly, as a Jew, Herbert Bierhoff has a responsibility to prevent the suffering of those children, possibly even against the wishes of the parents. At the least, he could have shared his knowledge with other parents, to let them make their own decisions. Instead Herbert Bierhoff kept his privileged information, and his merciful poison, to himself, horded it like a loaf of bread that might have nourished others.

Other questions, other nightmare scenarios, emerge: What if Herbert had several children, but only enough poison for one? What if he had no poison at all, how then could he "save" Ellen? If Herbert's action is acceptable, is it solely because of the circumstances and his method?

If we forgive Herbert for what he did do, can we forgive him for what he did *not* do?

This is the horrifying bind, the sickening awfulness, the fear and trembling, that follows if we pardon Herbert for killing his daughter: His action still results in the death of six million, and the unrivaled suffering of those who even temporarily survive. No child can be "saved" as Ellen is without subjecting parents and siblings to the same hellish choice Herbert faces.

That is a world without God, a world of moral paralysis.

Yet a world *with* God is no promise of life without dread or agony. As we know from the Torah, encountering God is always a harrowing, soul-shaking experience. When Jacob dreams of a ladder to heaven, he too is shaken, declaring, "Surely, God is in this place and I did not know it!" (Genesis 28:16). In his commentary on that event, W. Gunther Plaut observes of Jacob's descendants:

> They too will dream of angels and wondrous things,
> but when they awake and face the realities of the world
> they, too, will tremble and find the service of God filled
> with terror.

That certainly describes the world of the *Shoah*, the reality that Herbert finds himself in: dreams and nightmare realities.

It bears remembering that Jacob's father, Isaac, was almost killed by his father, Abraham. (It bears remembering, too, a paradox of the *Akeidah*, the binding of Isaac: Its moral result may be an affirmation of the sanctity of children, but that comes at the negation of Isaac's own childhood.) If we count Jacob as a patriarch, then we are descendants of Abraham and Isaac, and the *Akeidah* is family history. And that makes the Bierhoffs our family and our legacy as well. I must accept them as I do my father and my daughter.

As descendants so burdened, we do have the privilege of indicting our ancestor Herbert Bierhoff for his act, as we do with Abraham, saying in effect, God was in that place and he did not know it. But we dare not, because doing so exposes the alternative: God was in that place, in Ellen Bierhoff's bedroom, and we do not know it. After all, in the *Akeidah* story it is not only Isaac who is bound. Abraham, too, is bound, bound by and to God.

Once again, we can reach no verdict without accepting the unacceptable: The world is either Godless or else God sometimes requires parents to kill their children.

Perhaps where we find God in this story is with Ruth Bierhoff, Herbert's wife and Ellen's mother. She is the Sarah in this *Akeidah*, burdened with the knowledge of what her husband did to their child. In Ruth's deathbed dream, at the end of Act I (p. 26), Rachel, the Biblical matriarch, says the matter could only be judged on Earth. In her last words she asks, for "All possible judges, from the highest to the lowest on earth."

That dream and those words set in motion the judgment of Herbert Bierhoff. Shimon's pursuit exists because of them, and we are engaged in this discussion because of them. If we are to honor Ruth's suffering, if we are to value her experience as a survivor, then we are compelled to honor her demand, her dream, and judge Herbert. That is our test; our binding; our *Akeidah*. We are permitted to judge without either condemning or pardoning: "judgment" is also defined as "a statement of something believed"; in other words, judging is an assertion of belief, an act of faith by itself. To borrow the teaching of Rabbi Tarfon in *Ethics of the Fathers* (2:21), when we judge Herbert and judge Abraham—and thereby judge ourselves—we are not required to complete the task, to reach a verdict. Yet neither are we free to abstain from the duty, a duty and act of faith I will bear in mind whenever I remember my father, and whenever my daughter tells me her dreams.

171

SOURCES

The Torah, A Modern Commentary, ed. W. Gunther Plaut (New York: Union of American Hebrew Congregations, 1981).

Etz Hayim, eds. David Lieber, Chaim Potok, Harold Kushner, et. al. (New York: The Rabbinical Assembly, 2001).

Rabbi Joseph Telushkin, *Jewish Wisdom* (New York: William Morrow and Co., Inc, 1994).

The American Heritage Dictionary of the English Language, Fourth Edition (Boston: Houghton Mifflin, 2000).

Explanation, Understanding, and Holding Holocaust Perpetrators Responsible: The Myth of the Slippery Slope to Exculpation

David H. Jones

"**Shimon:** If I understand [Claude] Lanzmann correctly,
he argues that if you found a reason, it would almost
create a mitigating circumstance for the perpetrators.
Or, put another way: if indeed Hitler had a Jewish
grandfather, his perceived sense of shame at defiling his
racial purity would explain and might, in a totally
distorted sense, justify his hatred of the Jews. Thus, his
total war on the Jews might become almost rational,
even logical… Explaining leads to understanding, and
understanding leads to mitigating circumstances within
a certain mind-set. . . ."

The Judgment of Herbert Bierhoff[1]

"There are some pictures of Hitler as a baby, aren't there?
I think that there is even a book written by a
psychoanalyst about Hitler's childhood, an attempt at
explanation which is for me obscenity as such."

The Obscenity of Understanding:
An Evening with Claude Lanzmann[2]

---

[1] Sigi Ziering, *The Judgment of Herbert Bierhoff*, 32-33.
[2] Claude Lanzmann, "The Obscenity of Understanding: An Evening with Claude
Lanzmann," *American Imago* 48, no. 4 (1991): 480.

I. Introduction:

What I call "the myth of the slippery slope to exculpation" is the view that explanation inevitably leads to understanding, and understanding leads to excusing and exculpation. It is reflected in the old saying that to understand all is to forgive all. Of course, if this were in fact the truth, then one could understand why so many people, including an eminent artist like Claude Lanzmann, would have such a fear of any attempt to explain the personality and actions of Holocaust perpetrators like Hitler. But it really is a myth, and Lanzmann's fear is unjustified. No historical or psychological explanation of Hitler based on credible evidence has come even close to exculpating him for his horrendous crimes. There is a very good reason why this is so. The more we learn about Hitler, how he developed psychologically, how he freely created his own warped sense of personal identity, including his fanatical belief that he had a "divine mission" to exterminate the Jews, the more we see how fully blameworthy he is for his evil deeds. Far from exculpating Hitler, well-founded explanations actually incriminate him.[3]

My purpose in this essay is to show in some detail why the myth of the slippery slope to exculpation is indeed a myth. The myth survives in large part because the various relationships between explanation and moral responsibility are rather complex and easily misunderstood. Consequently, attempts to draw out the moral implications of historical and psychological explanations are often fraught with conceptual confusion, mistaken assumptions, and illogical inferences. I shall try to identify some of the most frequently encountered confusions and mistakes. In order to do this properly, it is necessary to pay considerably more attention to the ethics of responsibility and the psychology of morals than is sometimes done in writing about responsibility in the Holocaust.

The basic concept in the ethics of responsibility is individual responsibility, or as I will refer to it, blameworthiness; for this reason, it will be the focus of my discussion. Being blameworthy for having done something wrong means that one is justifiably liable to what I call "judgmental blame," that is, liable to being judged adversely, to being

---

[3] David H. Jones, *Moral Responsibility in the Holocaust* (Lanham, MD: Rowman & Littlefield, 1999), See especially chapter 6, "The Principal Perpetrator: Adolf Hitler".

disapproved of, and to being regarded as reprehensible by others, for what one has done. For a person to be fully blameworthy for having done something wrong, he or she must have done it (1) intentionally, (2) knowingly, (3) voluntarily, and (4) with a bad motive (or motives). The degree of judgmental blame that one deserves varies with the seriousness of the wrong act; with whether one acted intentionally, knowingly, and voluntarily; and with the badness of one's motives. Judgmental blame need not be expressed overtly; it consists essentially of how one judges the wrongdoer or what one feels about him or her, whether one expresses this explicitly or not. However, ordinarily, judgmental blame is also conveyed to the person who is regarded as blameworthy, whether in speech or other behavior, including what one might call informal moral sanctions such as withdrawal of love, affection, or friendship. If the person is regarded as highly blameworthy, these sanctions might include such drastic measures as a refusal to participate with him or her in cooperative activities, or even in a general shunning by the community. Some elements of blameworthiness are recognized in criminal law; for example, in most developed legal systems, people are liable to criminal punishment for committing an unlawful act only if they do so intentionally, with *mens rea* (a guilty mind).[4]

An all-important proviso in the ethics of responsibility is that blameworthiness (moral responsibility) does not follow automatically from wrongdoing alone. The four conditions for full blameworthiness guarantee this, especially (1), (2) and (3), each of which is a necessary condition. There are two main reasons why a person may not be blameworthy for committing a particular wrong act; he or she may have a justification (in which case the presumption that the act is wrong is overridden by reasons that make it at least all right to have done it, as, for example, when a police officer kills an armed fugitive who has taken hostages), or he or she may have a valid excuse (in which case, although the act is wrong, the person is not blameworthy for committing it, because one or more of the three necessary conditions are not present, as, for example, when a person kills someone purely by accident, neither intentionally nor negligently). The topic of this paper can be rephrased as the question whether historical and psychological explanations of the Holocaust start us down a slippery

---

[4] Jones, *Moral Responsibility*, chapter 1.

slope to exculpation because they inevitably establish that perpetrators have a justification or a valid excuse for their immoral acts. I shall argue that the answer is no, they do not.

However, there is another kind of reason that has sometimes been given to explain why perpetrators of the Holocaust committed their atrocious acts, which, if it were in fact true, would either completely exculpate them, or at least, drastically reduce their blameworthiness. This is the theory that the principal perpetrators, especially members of the Nazi party, the SS, and the Gestapo, were all suffering from a mental illness, a pathological "Nazi personality." The reason why this theory would exculpate the perpetrators is drastically different from the reason why a valid excuse exculpates. Unlike a valid excuse, which takes for granted that the wrongdoer is a competent moral agent with sufficient capacities for rational thought and self-control to be held accountable for his or her conduct, an explanation that invokes mental pathology automatically impugns the wrongdoer's status as a competent person. The wrongdoer is not only deemed not blameworthy, but (like an infant or an animal) non-responsible altogether. It is not difficult to understand why immediately after World War II, many professional psychologists and psychiatrists were drawn to the hypothesis of a Nazi personality, given the horror and extent of the recently discovered atrocities committed by the Nazi regime. However, years of intensive investigation failed to identify the existence of such a syndrome, and one recent study which reviewed the research concluded that no "diagnosable impairments that would account for their actions were found" among the subjects studied (which included the twenty-one main defendants in the Nuremberg trial, as well as many rank-and-file defendants who had participated in atrocities).[5] Consequently, I shall ignore this hypothesis in the remainder of my discussion.

My critical discussion of the myth of the slippery slope from explanation to exculpation is organized as follows: I start with historical explanations, because they tend to be the most general and abstract; I then turn to situational explanations in psychology, using Stanley

---

[5] Eric A. Zillmer, et al., *The Quest for the Nazi Personality: A Psychological Investigation of Nazi War Criminals* (Hillsdale, NJ: L. Erlbaum Associates, 1995), 96-100, 144.

Explanation, Understanding, and Holding Holocaust Perpetrators Responsible

Milgram's well-known studies of obedience as my main example; and finally I use the conclusions drawn from the previous sections to assess the blameworthiness of bureaucratic perpetrators, considered as a group, and then the blameworthiness of an individual perpetrator, Franz Stangl, who served as *Kommandant* of two death camps, Sobibor and Treblinka.

II. Historical Explanations and Exculpation:

The myth of the slippery slope is often conjoined with another dubious claim, namely, that the Holocaust itself is inexplicable. For example, Claude Lanzmann asserts that historical explanations for the Holocaust in fact fail to explain, because (at best) they give only necessary conditions. He insists that no matter how many such necessary conditions are included in the purported explanation, they will never be sufficient to explain the Holocaust; there remains "a gap, an *abyss*, and this abyss will never be bridged".[6] Unfortunately, Lanzmann does not support this strong claim with specific arguments. Of course, it is not difficult to understand why he might be inclined to hold such a strong view. Since he seems committed to the myth of the slippery slope, it is very plausible that he would also be drawn to a skeptical conclusion about the very possibility of explaining the Holocaust.

Other writers on the Holocaust have made very similar claims. For example, Nora Levin has stated that the Holocaust is "humanly incomprehensible," while Elie Wiesel has held that it "transcends history".[7] However, this judgment is not generally shared by historians, who tend to assume (correctly I believe) that the Holocaust, like any other event in human history, is explainable, at least in principle. Yehuda Bauer, for example, has declared that to deny this would be to retreat into "mysticism".[8] This does not mean that the historical explanations that

---

[6] Lanzmann, "Obscenity," 481.

[7] Dan Magurshak, "The "Incomprehensibility" of the Holocaust: Tightening up Some Loose Usage," in *Echoes from the Holocaust: Reflections on a Dark Time*, ed. Alan Rosenberg and Gerald E. Myers (Philadelphia: Temple University Press, 1988), Quoted by Magurshak on p. 421 of his article in which he criticizes the views expressed in them.

[8] Yehuda Bauer, "On the Place of the Holocaust in History," *Holocaust and Genocide Studies* 2, no. 2 (1987): 211.

are currently available are the last word, complete and free from error. Neither does it mean that we will necessarily attain a complete and irrefutable explanation at some time in the future. It only means that we have no reason to stop trying to increase our understanding of the Holocaust by continuing to search for more accurate and more comprehensive explanations.

Moreover, writers like Lanzmann seem to beg the question when they deny that an historical explanation can identify a sufficient condition for the occurrence of the Holocaust. Indeed, there seems to be a growing consensus among historians about the principal elements that constitute the correct explanation why the Holocaust occurred. Yehuda Bauer has succinctly summarized this explanation:

> The 'moderate antisemitism' of the bulk of the German people was absolutely essential. It prevented any effective opposition from taking place to the murder of an unpopular minority.
>
> It seems therefore that a political elite that had come to power with pseudo-messianic concepts of saving humanity from the Jews had used a broad stratum of intelligentsia which identified with it totally, to execute a murder program which went unopposed largely because a broad-based, in itself non-murderous antisemitism, had both prepared the way and then prevented any effective resistance. This is clearly shown by the fact that when the populace strongly opposed the regime's actions, such as in the case of the euthanasia program, the regime retreated. It did so, even when the Jews were involved—in Febuary 1943, a group of German wives of Jewish husbands protested publicly against the arrest and planned deportation of their men, and the Gestapo freed the men. In Berlin! In the middle of the war![9]

[9] Yehuda Bauer, "Is the Holocaust Explicable?" *Holocaust and Genocide Studies* 5, no. 2 (1990): 152.

In effect, Bauer claims that a combination of several factors, (1) a revolutionary Nazi elite fully committed to planning and ordering the complete extermination of all Jews under German control, so-called "true believers," (2) a broad stratum of the loyal intelligentsia (students, teachers, academics, medical doctors, lawyers, and other professionals) which would carry out the orders, and (3) the pervasive presence of a traditional moderate antisemitism among the mass of the German population, constituted a sufficient condition for the Holocaust to occur. Since these conditions remained virtually unchanged throughout the period from late 1941 to the end of 1944, there was nothing to stop the genocide.[10] Himmler did not order the gas chambers and crematoria in Auschwitz destroyed until November 1944. Although he may have been concerned about the rapid advance of Soviet armies from the east, he was also convinced that the killing of the Jews was virtually complete.[11]

Bauer does not claim that this historical explanation is either complete or irrefutable. He describes it as "a possible 'model' of explanation" which takes us a "certain distance in understanding the Holocaust, "but which "may have to be revised as research proceeds."[12] Still, if it is essentially correct, then it does identify the sufficient condition that in fact caused the Holocaust to occur. Moreover, this explanation has some very important implications. For example, if one or more of the individual factors that made up the sufficient condition had in fact not existed, the Holocaust would not have occurred. Moreover, if the complete set of conditions had lasted only six months, instead of four full years, the Holocaust would not have had anywhere near the five or six million victims that it actually claimed. In short, the explanation helps us see that the Holocaust, like any human event, was contingent on a complex set of conditions that were not inevitable and some of which might just as easily have been otherwise.

It is important to keep in mind that among the things that might have been otherwise are the choices and decisions made by millions of individual Germans who made up the three factors that constituted the

---

[10] Bauer, "Explicable?" 150-52.
[11] Raul Hilberg, The Destruction of the European Jews (New York London: Holmes & Meier, 1985), 980-81.
[12] Bauer, "Explicable?" 150.

sufficient condition: committed Nazis, loyal members of the intelligentsia, and the mass of the population. The more we learn about how these individual choices and decisions were made, the more we will understand how and why the Holocaust happened. Perhaps it is this possibility of increased understanding as we obtain more detailed information about how and why individual perpetrators chose to participate in the Holocaust, and why they continued their participation to the very end, that Lanzmann has in mind (however dimly) when he says there will always be "a gap" between the set of necessary historical conditions and the actual perpetration of the killings. If this is the point he is actually trying to make, his claim remains unconvincing, because there is no good reason to suppose that this kind of "gap" cannot (in principle) ever be closed. In any case, we know that it can be incrementally narrowed by each new investigation. If, as a matter of fact, the gap does not get completely closed (which is likely to be the case) it will be because the people involved have died taking their story with them, evidence has been destroyed, or for some other reason the relevant evidence is permanently unattainable. However, this mundane fact about the perishability and unattainability of some historical evidence hardly shows that there is something about the Holocaust that makes it inherently inexplicable.

While Bauer is surely correct when he states that an historical explanation takes us a certain distance in understanding why the Holocaust occurred, it is also clear that it does not explain how the individuals who belonged to the various groups in German society he mentions (the Nazi elite, the intelligentsia, and the mass of the population) made their choices. Consequently, it does not provide the specific information we need to make an ethical assessment of individual moral responsibility. This is a general problem with all historical, sociological, and group psychological explanations that are formulated either exclusively or preponderantly in terms of the behavior of institutions (i.e., governments, armies, parties, bureaucracies, etc.), whole societies, groups, or other social aggregates, rather than in terms of the behavior of individuals. In most cases, historical explanations tell us very little, if anything, about the motives, beliefs, and goals of the many thousands, indeed millions, of individuals who took part in the events being explained, or about how they made their choices and decisions. Thus, they would at best form only part of a complete explanation, supposing that one were ever arrived at.

Explanation, Understanding, and Holding Holocaust Perpetrators Responsible

In summary, historical explanation can give us increased understanding of the Holocaust, including what appears to be the sufficient condition for its occurrence. However, it is highly unlikely that historical explanations lead us down a slippery slope to inevitable exculpation of the perpetrators of the Holocaust for the simple reason that most of them do not provide sufficiently detailed and relevant information about individuals whose actions we might want to assess from an ethical point of view. They neither incriminate nor exculpate. Thus, I conclude that the nature of historical explanation does not support the myth of the slippery slope.

III. Situational Explanations in Psychology: Milgram's Obedience Experiments:

A. Justifications, Excuses, and Mitigating Circumstances

Experimental studies in psychology can also increase our understanding of how the Holocaust happened, however, when they are designed primarily to study the influence of the situation on behavior, they usually shed very little, if any, light on the reasons why individuals act the way they do. Consequently, these studies are unlikely to shed very much light on the blameworthiness of the individual subjects who participate in them. Nonetheless, Stanley Milgram's famous experimental studies of obedience are often used to try to help explain why most perpetrators participated in the Holocaust, obediently following orders and bureaucratic routine. Milgram's experiments established that about two-thirds of his subjects, who had been assigned the role of "teacher," would continue to administer what they believed were extremely painful high-voltage shocks to a "learner" (in actuality a confederate of the experimenter), even after the "learner" cried out in pain, pleaded for the experiment to stop, and then became silent and unresponsive.[13] Milgram's experiments show that the situation in which individuals find themselves often plays a powerful role in determining how they will behave. Most disturbing is the finding that most people can be induced to act contrary

---

[13] Stanley Milgram, *Obedience to Authority: An Experimental View* (New York: Harper Colophon, 1974); John Sabini and Maury Silver, *Moralities of Everyday Life* (New York: Oxford University Press, 1982), 57-71.

to their beliefs about right and wrong. Many of Milgram's subjects who continued to shock the "learner" up to the (ostensibly) highest level of voltage also expressed concern about whether it was right to continue, showed evident signs of deep distress, or repeatedly asked that the experiment be stopped.

Milgram ran the obedience experiment in a number of different ways, changing the specific features of the situation to see what difference this would make in the way individuals responded. One important variable turned out to be the distance of the "teacher" from the "learner." Thus, when the "teacher" was required to place the hand of the "learner" directly on a shock plate, subjects showed great stress while obedience up to the highest level of shock fell to 20 percent; but when the "teacher" was completely removed from the vicinity of the "learner" and got all information from verbal designations on the machine, subjects showed little stress and there was virtually complete obedience.[14] In another variation, Milgram used actor\collaborators together with naïve subjects to ascertain the effect of peer pressure on obedience. He found that peer pressure could either reinforce obedience or bolster the individual's capacity to resist authority, depending on the opinions expressed by the actor\collaborators.[15]

As I have noted, Milgram's situational explanations have been used to help explain how some perpetrators were influenced to obey authoritative orders to kill Jews in the Holocaust.[16] There is plenty of evidence that many perpetrators, especially bureaucratic "desk murderers," found themselves in situations in which authoritative orders, bureaucratic routine, peer pressure, and "distance" from the killing combined to make it relatively easy for them to make an essential contribution to the killing with few pangs of conscience.[17]

Thus, there is little doubt that Milgram's studies increase our understanding of how the Holocaust might actually have happened. However, just as with Bauer's historical explanation, applying Milgram's

---

[14] Sabini and Silver, *Moralities of Everyday Life*, 60.
[15] Stanley Milgram, "Group Pressure and Action Against a Person," *Journal of Abnormal and Social Psychology* 9 (1964): 137-43.
[16] Sabini and Silver, *Moralities of Everyday Life*, is a good example.
[17] Hilberg, *The Destruction of the European Jews*, 1010-29.

findings about his experimental subjects directly to the question of the blameworthiness of perpetrators of the Holocaust is problematical. We can see this most clearly by looking more closely at what Milgram's findings imply, if anything, about the blameworthiness of the subjects in his studies, a question that Milgram did not address. In particular, we need to know in more detail how individual subjects interacted with the situation. Were they passive victims exposed to the pernicious "influence" of the situation, having little or no control over how it affected them? Or were they, perhaps, in varying degrees receptive to its influence, perhaps even actively contributing to the outcome, namely, continuing to shock the "learner" and avoiding a confrontation with the investigator who insists they must continue? In short, we need to know more about the subjects' thoughts and feelings as they continued and, most importantly, how and why they made the choice to obey or not to obey. If we can arrive at some answers to these questions, we may be better able to see what Milgram's experiments imply regarding the blameworthiness of Holocaust perpetrators.

Being quite aware that his experimental findings raise as many questions as they answer, Milgram offered some general hypotheses that might explain why individual subjects in his experiments obey the instruction to continue administering what they believe are increasingly painful electric shocks to a helpless "learner." These hypotheses include the following: that (1) there is an evolutionary bias that favors adaptability to social hierarchies and organized activity, (2) subjects feel an obligation to continue because they volunteered for the experiment, (3) people accept the legitimacy of science in general because its purpose is good, (4) people accept the legitimacy of the "psychological experiment" in particular for the same reason, (5) people are reluctant to disobey or question the instructions to continue because they have been socialized to defer to superior authority, and would be embarrassed to object, and (6) people tend to see themselves as agents of the scientific experimenter who has the responsibility for the safety and well-being of the learner.[18]

For purposes of my analysis, I shall assume that each of these hypotheses might possibly be true; indeed, each of them seems intuitively plausible and consistent with commonsense understanding of biological and psychological facts. In addition, I shall suppose that all of them, or

---

[18] Milgram, *Obedience*, 135-47.

most of them, apply to a particular individual taking part in Milgram's experiment, that is, they provide either the whole of, or a substantial part of the true explanation why he or she obeyed the instructions to continue with the experiment. Finally, I shall assume (what I believe is in fact true) that it was morally wrong to continue to administer what one believed to be severe electric shocks to a helpless learner who cried out in pain, repeatedly asked for the experiment to end, etc., and that (like nearly all of Milgram's subjects) this particular experimental subject knew that it was wrong, or at least highly questionable. My main interest in this example is to try to answer the following question: If we suppose that Milgram's hypotheses provide the true explanation why this subject continued to deliver shocks, knowing that it was wrong or questionable to do so, what would that imply, if anything, about his or her moral responsibility or blameworthiness?

Before I can address this question properly, I need to introduce some additional distinctions in the ethics of responsibility. Recall the general principle noted earlier: moral responsibility or blameworthiness does not follow automatically from the fact of wrongdoing alone. Ordinarily, when people do something wrong, we may reasonably infer that they are blameworthy for having done it. However, if they have either a justification or a valid excuse, this inference is blocked; they are blameless for their wrongdoing. On the other hand, if there is only a mitigating circumstance, the degree of their blameworthiness is reduced. For example, the obedient subject might have been justified in inflicting painful electric shocks in order to treat a mental patient suffering from brain seizures. In effect, a justification shows the act is not wrong, but right, all things considered. By contrast, the obedient subject would have had a valid excuse if he or she had been coerced by a threat of severe punishment for failing to comply with the instructions to continue. The reason is that people do not have a duty to deliberately sacrifice themselves for the sake of another person, although it would be admirable and praiseworthy if they voluntarily did so. A person who is obedient under coercion acts permissibly; what they do is "all right." Thus, unlike a justification, a valid excuse does not show that obedience is actually right; instead, it shows that the person is not blameworthy for what is indeed a morally undesirable act. An example of a merely mitigating circumstance is the fact that subjects in Milgram's experiments were assured that the "learner" would not suffer any permanent physical injury.[19] The fact that the obedient subject was given this assurance means that he or she was not guilty of intentionally risking the "learner's" life or long-term physical well-being. Although he or she may still be blameworthy for intentionally causing the "learner" (ostensibly) severe pain, the degree of blame is less than that which might have been deserved otherwise.

With these basic distinctions in hand, I can rephrase my main question: assuming that Milgram's hypotheses provide the true explanation for why the subject continued to deliver electric shocks, do they also (either individually or in combination) provide a justification, valid excuse, or mitigating circumstance that blocks or lessens blameworthiness? I think that it is safe to say that none of them, either individually or collectively, provides a justification. Consider (1), the evolutionary bias that favors adaptability to social hierarchies and organized activity. The fact that all human beings are born with a trait that makes them to some degree disposed to adapt to the requirements of social hierarchy and organization says something about our shared capacity for living in society, but it says nothing at all about ethical questions such as which hierarchies and organizations are good or just, nor anything about which social activities we ought, or ought not, to engage in. Moreover, if "adaptability" is just a fancy name for a propensity to "get along by going along," a notorious character defect, it does nothing at all to provide a justification for continued obedience of the subject. Similar observations apply to (5), the fact that people have been socialized to defer to superior authority. It must be admitted that in contrast with (1), (5) at least opens up the possibility of some plausible justifications. For example, in some kinds of situations, individuals may properly justify their obedience by appealing to the fact that they were only following legitimate and authoritative orders. Thus, the laws of war grant immunity to soldiers who are ordered by their superiors to open fire on the enemy in battle; everything else being equal, they are immune to criminal prosecution for any deaths they cause. Moreover, in many cases this explanation is also a valid excuse that renders them morally blameless. Of course, it is notorious that all too often soldiers are ordered to commit war crimes, ethnic cleansing, and genocide. This is why the qualifying expression, "legitimate orders,"

---

[19] Milgram, *Obedience*, 176-77.

is necessary. There is one very telling consideration against the trait described in (5); this trait is usually referred to as authoritarianism, because its salient feature is the disposition to defer to superior authority instead of thinking for oneself. If anything, such a disposition is as likely as not to lead to moral obtuseness and wrongdoing.

Perhaps enough has already been said about the questionable moral value of authoritarianism to indicate why neither (3), accepting the legitimacy of science, nor (4), accepting the legitimacy of the experiment, could supply reliable justifications. As for (2), the fact that one volunteered should not justify continued obedience even in the subject's own mind, once he or she had reached the point when serious doubts arose about the legitimacy of the "learning" experiment itself. Much less does it provide an objective justification that would make continued obedience right. Finally, (6), the tendency to see oneself as a passive agent of the experimenter to whom one ascribes total responsibility for everything that occurs, including ones own conduct, is hardly admirable. Indeed, it could serve as a paradigm of blameworthy self-deception. No person has the power to unilaterally renounce all personal moral responsibility for his or her own actions and shift it to someone else. Consequently, the fact that this tendency helps to explain why the subject was obedient does nothing to show that it was right to obey.

Do any of Milgram's hypotheses provide a valid excuse? Unlike a justification, a valid excuse does not show that continued obedience was right; instead, it presupposes that obedience was wrong, but exculpates the person as blameless for doing it. Again, neither (1), biologically evolved social adaptability, nor (5), having been socialized to defer to superior authority, provide a valid excuse that would make the subject blameless. In fact, the only remotely plausible ground on which it might be argued that (1) and (5) are excusing conditions would be if they each rendered the subject powerless to refrain from obedience; that is, if these tendencies operated rather like an "irresistible impulse" beyond the subject's control. If this were in fact true, then the subject could claim that he or she lacked the ability to do otherwise; it was impossible not to obey. However, there is no biological or psychological evidence that evolution and socialization produce such an irresistible urge to obedience; the most one can say is that they create a tendency to obey. Granted that in some people the tendency might be quite strong, in most people it is a tendency that is

routinely overridden. In fact, in the standard version of Milgram's
"learning" experiment, approximately one-third of the subjects refused
to continue shocking the "learner." At most, (1) and (5) might be
mitigating circumstances that lessen blame if they made it to some degree
difficult for the subject to disobey. Very similar observations can be made
about (3) and (4); since both of them might make it somewhat difficult,
though not impossible, to doubt the goodness of science or to challenge
the experimenter, or both, they could mitigate blame. I am inclined to
argue that neither (2), the fact that one volunteered, nor (6), shifting all
responsibility to the experimenter, constitute valid excuses, for the same
kinds of reasons that I rejected them as justifications. Indeed, it is difficult
to see how the fact that one volunteered to engage in an activity that
turns out to be morally wrong, or at least questionable, could serve either
as a valid excuse or as a mitigating circumstance. As I have already pointed
out, no person has the power to shift all responsibility for his or her own
conduct to someone else. Moreover, convincing oneself that this may
justifiably be done is a paradigm of blameworthy self-deception used to
evade responsibility.[20]

In summary, this review of Milgram's hypotheses shows that, taken
either singly or in combination, they fail to provide either a justification or
a valid excuse for a subject's wrongful obedience. At most, some of them
might constitute mitigating circumstances that lessen blame. There might
be a few individuals, to whom a combination of several of the mitigating
circumstances applies, lessening their degree of blameworthiness in an
additive fashion, but there is no reason to think that this would ever amount
to complete exculpation. Thus, even if we were to accept Milgram's
hypotheses as providing the true explanation of why so many of his subjects
were obedient, this would not start us down a slippery slope to exculpation.

B. How to Lower the Standard for Blameworthiness Without Really
Trying: Find Out How Most People Behave.

Another source of confusion in our thinking about the relationship
between explanation and responsibility is the tendency to make
questionable inferences about the blameworthiness of individuals based

---

[20] Jones, *Moral Responsibility*, Chapter 4, "Self-"Deception.

solely on how their behavior compares with what many or most people do in similar circumstances. The underlying assumption is that individuals who behave the way that most people behave, even when this involves wrongdoing, are either not blameworthy at all, or, if it is admitted that they are to some extent blameworthy, they are deemed to be comparatively no worse and no better than most other people, so their blameworthiness does not deserve any special notice, much less opprobrium. This way of thinking can also be illustrated using the results of Milgram's initial obedience experiment. Recall that about two-thirds of his subjects obeyed the instructions to shock the "learner" to the (ostensibly) highest level of voltage, while one-third disobeyed at some point below that. Now one way to interpret this finding is to infer that, although most of the compliant subjects believed (correctly, I have argued) that their continued obedience was grievously wrong, they were, nonetheless, not seriously blameworthy for continuing. How is this ethical judgment reached? The crucial inference is this: since two-thirds of the subjects failed to disobey, it must be objectively exceedingly difficult or practically impossible to disobey, therefore, it is unreasonable to expect, much less require, people to disobey. We know from Milgram's account that most of the compliant subjects actually wanted very badly to stop delivering shocks. Since each of the subjects had a strong motive for disobeying (so this reasoning goes), one may infer that the main reason why they failed to translate that desire into action that would end the experiment (for example, by explicitly expressing their refusal to continue) was that they found it very difficult or virtually impossible to do so. Thus, one may infer that it is objectively virtually impossible for anyone to obey in those circumstances.

The next step in this way of thinking is to argue that since the correct explanation why two-thirds of the subjects continued to obey was because it was objectively very difficult to refuse to obey, any individual who failed to disobey was either blameless or, since they behaved no better and no worse than most people, only slightly blameworthy. It is this inference that clearly differentiates this way of thinking from the previous inquiry into whether Milgram's hypotheses provide a justification, a valid excuse, or a mitigating circumstance. The inference to the comparative blamelessness of each individual is made without any reference to whether his or her behavior is explained by Milgram's hypotheses. It is also made without any reference to how much or how little reflection, effort, and self-control the individual exercised while trying to act on his or her desire to stop the experiment. In effect, this way of thinking determines the moral standard for assessing the blameworthiness of conduct by the use of a single criterion: how do most people in fact behave? The inevitable effect is the ethical equivalent of the "dumbing down" of learning standards in education: the standard for blameworthy conduct is lowered to accommodate what most people in fact do.

However, using this single criterion ignores the very real possibility that many of the obedient subjects may not have made much of an effort to resist the instructions to continue with the experiment. It is not at all unusual for people who in fact have the ability to do something to fail to use their powers of practical reasoning, deliberation, and self-control properly and fully. It begs the question to assume that all of the obedient subjects in fact made a maximum effort, using all of their moral capacities to the fullest, to stop the experiment. In the absence of evidence to the contrary, it seems just as plausible to assume that many, perhaps most, of the obedient subjects did not make a maximum effort. If this were in fact the correct explanation why they failed to stop the experiment, then those subjects would be to some extent blameworthy. Why? Because it was wrong for them to continue giving shocks, they knew that it was wrong, they had the ability to stop, but they did not try, or if they tried, they did not try hard enough. They had a duty to refrain from inflicting severe pain on an (ostensibly) unwilling "learner," even if it would have been difficult to refrain. After all, what function does ethics have if not to set standards of good behavior that may in fact be difficult, though not impossible, to meet?

Most puzzling of all, this way of thinking would also ignore the highly relevant fact that a third of the subjects successfully disobeyed. If one out of three subjects were able to disobey, then disobedience was more than a remote possibility, it was in fact quite feasible, however difficult some subjects may have found it. What is the explanation why a third of the subjects managed to overcome the difficulty while two-thirds did not? Would the correct explanation exculpate or incriminate the obedient subjects? Interestingly, Milgram did not raise these questions, which might have led him away from his preoccupation with the power of the situation to determine behavior. For example, he might have studied the subjects who disobeyed to see if they shared any individual traits that obedient subjects lacked, individual traits that might help explain the difference in their behavior.

The kinds of traits that Milgram might have discovered are suggested by the results obtained by Samuel and Pearl Oliner when they addressed an analogous question about the difference between the character traits of people who rescued Jews during the Holocaust and those who did not.[21]

They studied a large sample of rescuers and compared them with a similar-sized sample of people who had not been rescuers and found that rescuers were much more likely to have feelings of compassion and a sense of duty toward other people who need help, regardless of whether they belong to one's own social group or not (a complex psychological trait that the Oliners called "extensivity").[22] Indeed, the Oliners found that this difference was statistically significant; there was a 70 percent probability that a person who had the traits of extensivity would also be a rescuer. So it is reasonable to conclude that the possession of these traits explains, in whole or in part, why these people rescued Jews, and that the absence of these traits explains why people did not rescue Jews.

The Oliners' findings have significant implications for the comparative blameworthiness of rescuers and non-rescuers. In ethics, the two traits that the Oliners refer to as extensivity, compassion and a sense of duty to help others, are both recognized as virtues, that is, traits of good character that make a person admirable and worthy of respect. Correspondingly, people who lack these traits of good character altogether, are deemed to suffer from a moral defect, and are, thus, disreputable. Even people who have these virtues, but in a weak or truncated form, are to some degree less deserving of respect. Moreover, when people's defects of character lead them to do something wrong, either by act or omission, their wrong acts reflect the defects from which they flow, thus making the people blameworthy. Consequently, people who did not rescue Jews during the Holocaust solely because they lacked good character (i.e., they had no valid excuse or justification for not helping, but refrained because they had little or no compassion for Jews, or they had little or no sense of duty to help, or both) were to some extent blameworthy (i.e., responsible) for

---

[21] Samuel P. Oliner and Pearl M. Oliner, *The Altruistic Personality: Rescuers of Jews in Nazi Germany* (New York and London: The Free Press, 1988).
[22] Oliner and Oliner, *Altruistic Personality*, 249.

their failure to help.[23] It would be manifestly absurd and self-defeating for them to plead lack of virtue as an excuse for wrongdoing. To the contrary, this explanation why they did not help Jews would incriminate them; it would show them to be people lacking in ordinary decency and good character. The Oliners' findings are another confirmation of my general thesis that there is no slippery slope from explanation to exculpation.

It seems more than plausible that there is an analogous explanation why one-third of Milgram's subjects disobeyed when fully two-thirds obeyed instructions to the end, namely, the subjects who disobeyed either had compassion for, or a sense of duty to give help to, the "learner" being shocked, whereas, those who obeyed lacked both of those traits, or had them in a very weak or truncated form. If so, then subjects who obeyed to the end are to some extent blameworthy for their failure to stop the experiment. Like people who failed to help or rescue Jews in the Holocaust without justification or excuse, their wrongful acts of omission reveal the moral defects in their character. Of course, I cannot prove that a lack of virtue is the correct explanation, in part, because Milgram was not interested in finding out why so many of his subjects did what they believed was right despite the supposed "power of the situation to determine behavior."

IV. The Blameworthiness of Holocaust Perpetrators

I want to turn now to an assessment of the blameworthiness of Holocaust perpetrators, using, among other considerations, the conclusions I have drawn from my analysis of Milgram's obedience experiments. Before I start this assessment, a few warnings and qualification are in order. It is not possible to make generalizations about the moral character (good, bad, or indifferent) of all members of institutions, bureaucracies, and other social groups, both because we do not have adequate information to make such an assessment, and (more importantly) because, even if we had the relevant information, it would force us realize that individual perpetrators did not fit into a single mold. However, there are two kinds of judgments we can sometimes make when we have the relevant information. First, if we know a lot about the situation in which most members of a group of perpetrators found themselves, about the typical decisions and choices they had to

---

[23] Jones, *Moral Responsibility*, chapter 9.

make, as well as about the kinds of actions that the group committed, we can justifiably infer the existence of several types of individuals among that group of perpetrators, individuals who differed in moral character (virtues and vices), in the motives for their actions, and in the justifications and\or excuses they did or did not have available, and so on.[24]

Thus, the first kind of judgment that we can sometimes make is to gauge the comparative blameworthiness of different kinds of perpetrators within a group. I shall use bureaucratic perpetrators as my example for this first kind of judgment.

The second kind of judgment we can sometimes make is an assessment of the moral character and blameworthiness of an individual perpetrator about whom we have a great deal of relevant information. I shall use the example of Franz Stangl, who is the subject of Gitta Sereny's book, *Into That Darkness: An Examination of Conscience*.[25]

A. Bureaucratic Perpetrators

The thousands of perpetrators in this category played an essential role in the implementation of the Final Solution, even if most of them were not directly involved in killing Jews. They were not required to shoot the victims beside a burial pit or herd them into the gas chambers; in fact, most of them were far removed from the scenes of horror. They were faceless bureaucrats in government offices, personnel of the state railway, or members of the police. There is plenty of evidence that most of them knew or strongly suspected that the Jews were in fact being systematically killed, and that they knew this was a deeply immoral. Toward the end of his majesterial three-volume history, *The Destruction of the European Jews*, Raul Hilberg discusses several explanations for the ability of bureaucratic perpetrators' to overcome what should have been a major obstacle to their participation in genocide, namely,

> ...the feeling of growing uneasiness that pervaded the bureaucracy from the lowest strata to the highest. That

---

[24] Jones, *Moral Responsibility*, 165-67.
[25] Gitta Sereny, *Into That Darkness: An Examination of Conscience* (New York: Vintage Books, 1983).

uneasiness was the product of moral scruples—the lingering effect of two thousand years of Western morality and ethics. A Western bureaucracy had never before faced such chasm between moral precepts and administrative action: an administrative machine had never been burdened with such a drastic task. In a sense the task of destroying the Jews put the German bureaucracy to a supreme test. The German technocrats solved also that problem and passed also this test.[26]

Nazi leaders like Heinrich Himmler, who was in charge of the Final Solution, regarded such moral scruples as "the weaknesses" of Christian morality that would have to be overcome.[27]

In a remarkable section entitled, "Psychological Problems," Hilberg provides a detailed analysis of the methods and tactics used by bureaucratic institutions, as well as the individuals working in them, which explains how these moral scruples were successfully overcome. His explanations of how and why bureaucratic perpetrators obediently complied with what they either knew, or strongly suspected, were immoral orders correspond to the explanations offered by Milgram for the obedience of most of his subjects. Hilberg divides his explanations into two kinds that he calls "mechanisms of repression"[28] and a "system of rationalizations."[29] Although Hilberg's description seems to suggest otherwise, the mechanisms of repression are not individual psychological processes. Rather, they are the institutional measures taken to make the bureaucratic destructive machine highly efficient and to make it easier for individual bureaucrats to cope with the reality of what they were doing: killing thousands, indeed millions, of Jews. These measures included secrecy—outsiders were kept ignorant— mandatory participation by insiders—everyone who knew was made to participate—prohibition of criticism—by both outsiders and insiders— prohibition of explicit conversation about the destructive process by insiders, and avoidance of explicit reference to "killing" and "killing operations" by

---

[26] Hilberg, *The Destruction of the European Jews*, 1010-11.
[27] Hilberg, *The Destruction of the European Jews*, 1009.
[28] Hilberg, *The Destruction of the European Jews*, 1012-17.
[29] Hilberg, *The Destruction of the European Jews*, 1017-29.

the use of euphemisms (e.g., *Sonderbehandlung*, 'special treatment,' instead of killing) in all correspondence.

The institutional measures of repression correspond roughly to the situational factors in Milgram's obedience experiments that supposedly determined the obedience of the "teacher" delivering electric shocks to the "learner." As Hilberg notes, bureaucratic perpetrators of the Final Solution were not supposed to look to the right or to the left; they were supposed to be totally immersed in the job at hand, fully implicated in it, with little or no opportunity to dwell on, much less raise doubts about, the nature of what they were doing. Everything in their situation would be designed to keep their minds on the immediate task and free from any distractions, especially any stimulus that would arouse conscious reflection on what they were doing. Nevertheless, Hilberg notes, these institutional measures were not sufficient to hide the killing "from the inner self…the bureaucracy was not spared an open encounter with its conscience."[30]

In short, while the institutional measures may have made the process more efficient, they actually did little, if anything, to quiet the uneasiness of perpetrators' consciences and prevent feelings of guilt. The perpetrators' were fully aware of the genocide in which they were participating; they could not plead an excuse of ignorance. At most, some of them might have been able to argue that the institutional measures provided mitigating circumstances that lessened their blameworthiness to some extent.

The system of rationalizations was intended to make it easier for individuals to quiet their own conscience. This system included first of all, an elaborate official justification for the killing process as a whole. Old conceptions about the Jew, reinforced and expanded by more recent Nazi ideology and propaganda, had developed into a mythological image of "international Jewry" that contained three main elements: It was a world-wide conspiracy plotting the destruction of Germany, it involved an inherently criminal people, and this people was an inferior form of life or vermin.[31] This justification was supposed to explain why "the Jew" had to be destroyed. Since this official justification was continuously presented as objective truth, it constituted yet another situational factor that was designed to make it easier for bureaucratic perpetrators to follow

---

[30] Hilberg, *The Destruction of the European Jews*, 1017.
[31] Hilberg, *The Destruction of the European Jews*, 1017-24.

their orders. However, according to Hilberg, this official ideological justification conveyed through continuous propaganda did not fully convince bureaucratic perpetrators. "They realized the connection between their paperwork and the heaps of corpses in the East, and they also realized the shortcomings of arguments that placed all evil on the Jew and all good on the German."[32] Thus, if Hilberg is correct, we can conclude that none of the situational factors in his explanation (neither the institutional measures nor the official ideological justification) provide a valid excuse for all bureaucratic perpetrators. For example, they could not plead the valid excuse of non-culpable ignorance, because, in fact, they knew too much.

By contrast, there were several other widely used rationalizations whose function was not to justify the killing process as a whole, but rather to justify the participation of individual perpetrators. Hilberg discusses five categories of these rationalizations.[33]

(1) The doctrine of superior orders was the favorite rationalization. Perpetrators claimed that they had a duty to follow legitimate orders. Sometimes this claim was intended to serve as a justification, on the ground that it would have been wrong to disobey. Since German political culture at that time was highly authoritarian, one can assume that some (many?) perpetrators truly believed this; if so, they might be excusable on the ground of non-culpable ignorance of the immorality of their participation. However, Hilberg gives several examples of disobedient perpetrators, including some high level ones, thus undermining the simplistic view that all Germans were mindless robots. Even more interesting is the fact that these disobedient perpetrators were not routinely given harsh punishment either; indeed, often nothing happened to them.[34] This fact throws doubt on the claim often made by perpetrators, namely, that they had no choice but to obey orders because they faced severe punishment or death for disobedience. If true, this would have been a valid excuse. Even if it had been true in some cases, Hilberg's account gives us a good reason to reject any blanket excuse of coercion for all bureaucratic perpetrators. Finally, some perpetrators used the doctrine of superior orders to absolve themselves of all responsibility and to shift it

---

[32] Hilberg, *The Destruction of the European Jews*, 1024.
[33] Hilberg, *The Destruction of the European Jews*, 1024-29.
[34] Hilberg, *The Destruction of the European Jews*, 1024-25.

upward to their superiors. I have already pointed out that no individual has the moral power to unilaterally reject accountability for his or her own actions. Even if perpetrators' superior officers explicitly assumed personal responsibility for the killings they ordered, thereby creating legal immunity for them, this would not be sufficient to make the subordinate morally blameless. At most it might serve as a mitigating factor.

(2) Perpetrators often claimed that their motives for participating in the Final Solution were not reprehensible; they did not act out of personal vindictiveness or hatred. To the contrary, many perpetrators insisted that they had actually helped Jews with good deeds.[35] In general, a person's motives for intentional and voluntary wrongdoing can at best aggravate or mitigate the degree of blameworthiness; in particular, good motives cannot serve as a valid excuse that makes one blameless. Thus, even if perpetrators' claims about the goodness of their motives were true, that would hardly absolve them of all blame for participating in genocide. Later, I shall complicate my assessment of blameworthiness by considering the high likelihood that perpetrators were often culpably self-deceived about their motives.

(3) The very nature of the often large and impersonal bureaucracies that were engaged in carrying out the Final Solution meant that the overall task was divided among disparate agencies, with a resulting general diffusion of responsibility. Thus, it was comparatively easy for individual perpetrators to view their own actions as non-criminal and to lay the blame on others. Bureaucrats who signed papers, railroad officials who scheduled deportation trains, and police who rounded up Jews and loaded them on the trains, could each plausibly (though mistakenly) claim that what they did was not criminal. After all, they argued, they did not kill anyone.[36] These lame excuses probably made it easier psychologically for the perpetrators to overcome their moral scruples, but from an ethical point of view, they are worthless. The millions of murders in the Final Solution could never have been carried out so successfully without the essential contribution of thousands of bureaucratic perpetrators who identified, arrested, and deported the Jewish victims. No bureaucrats, no Final Solution; its as simple as that.

---

[35] Hilberg, *The Destruction of the European Jews*, 1025-27.
[36] Hilberg, *The Destruction of the European Jews*, 1027-28.

(4) A closely related rationalization was built on the thought that precisely because there were so many others involved in the Final Solution, one was really powerless to make any difference. If one refused to participate, there were always others ready to take one's place.[37] This rationalization overlooks two things. First, many people did in fact find ways to "drop out," without anything happening to them (as Hilberg notes). Second, an act of omission (which would not have necessarily involved heroic self-sacrifice) would have been a good thing to do, even if it made no difference in the number of victims killed. Such an act of refraining need not have been cowardly or unfeeling, either; it could be the purest expression of personal integrity.

(5) The "last ditch psychological defense" of some perpetrators was what Hilberg sarcastically calls "the jungle theory," a simplistic version of Social Darwinism that was used especially by the Nazi elite, including both Hitler and Himmler.

> Himmler remembered this theory when he addressed
> the mobile killing personnel at Minsk. He told them to
> look at nature. Wherever they would look, they would
> find combat. They would find it among animals and
> among plants. Whoever tired of the fight went under.[38]

Of course, the trouble with such a theory is that it either proves too much (since every combatant in every war or conflict can make exactly the same observation with equal validity, or invalidity); or else it proves too little (since from the fact, if it is a fact, that combat is unavoidable, nothing at all follows about which nation, or cause, or ideology ought to win, or about whether an individual's participation is right or wrong). In short, the "theory" is really evidence of a deep conceptual confusion that has no consistent ethical implications at all. Hilberg is, thus, quite right to treat it with derision. The fact that some perpetrators used the jungle theory not only reflects badly on their moral character, but it also calls into question their sanity.

---

[37] Hilberg, *The Destruction of the European Jews*, 1028-29.
[38] Hilberg, *The Destruction of the European Jews*, 1029.

An especially important consideration in making an assessment of the blameworthiness of bureaucratic perpetrators is their use of psychological tactics of self-deception. Hilberg takes for granted that self-deception was a major factor in the ability of perpetrators to overcome their moral scruples.[39] He makes clear that perpetrators were far from being passive victims of the institutional measures of repression and official ideology, which were, in any case, insufficient to prevent feelings of guilt. Perpetrators succeeded in overcoming their moral scruples only by actively engaging in extensive tactics of self-deception in order to evade self-acknowledgment of the full truth of what they were doing. By remaining willfully ignorant, they hoped to evade responsibility for their essential role in the Final Solution. One can more fully appreciate why using self-deception made perpetrators even more blameworthy by looking closely at the nature of self-deception and how it works.

The kind of self-deception used by perpetrators is a very common psychological activity that nearly everyone engages at one time of another.[40] It consists of various tactics that enable us to evade acknowledging something to ourselves that would cause us fear, anxiety, guilt, or shame if we were to look at it honestly and squarely. For example, many of us evade thinking about our own death, or about all of the evil in the world, because it makes us anxious or depressed. The subjects about which we deceive ourselves are almost endlessly varied, but one principal subject about which almost everyone is at least tempted to engage in self-deception is our own conduct and character. After all, one of the strongest motives in human nature, a close competitor with the desire for self-preservation, is the need for self-respect. This is the desire that motivated most of the perpetrators who engaged in self-deceptive evasion of acknowledging the truth about their own role in the Final Solution. To have fully acknowledged to themselves that they were blameworthy for their essential part in killing thousands of Jews would have caused most of them deep feelings of guilt and shame, together with anxiety about the growing likelihood that they would be tried and punished by the Allies.[41] Like most people, they were very strongly motivated to avoid taking full

---

[39] Hilberg, *The Destruction of the European Jews*, 1029.
[40] Jones, *Moral Responsibility*, chapter 4.
[41] Hilberg, *The Destruction of the European Jews*, 522-23.

responsibility for their own actions, especially given the horrendous nature of what they were doing.

The tactics of self-deception they used to evade feeling guilty and responsible about their participation in the Final Solution would have included (1) avoiding explicitly thinking about Jews being killed, the methods of killing, the disposal of bodies, etc., (2) studiously avoiding noticing any relevant evidence that Jews were being killed, etc., and making no inquiries to find out what was in fact going on, (3) if relevant evidence (e.g., trainloads of used clothing arriving from the East) could not be avoided, immediately turning one's attention to other matters, (4) continually looking for evidence that confirmed more acceptable beliefs, such as the official cover story that the Jews really were being sent to the East to work, (5) and when (inevitably) one could no longer doubt that the Jews were being killed, rehearsing the various rationalizations identified by Hilberg about superior orders, one's own good motives, powerlessness, etc., to salve one's conscience. The institutional measures of repression were designed, of course, to make evasive self-deception easier; but one had to be actively and continuously engaged in these various tactics for the project to succeed. Even then, because the resulting state of self-deception was exceedingly fragile, doubts and feelings of guilt could erupt at any time. It is a mistake to think that most perpetrators were able to attain a state of blissful ignorance by self-deception. While some perpetrators, most notably Hitler, succeeded in achieving a state of self-deception that was invulnerable to contrary evidence, most perpetrators had to work very hard at maintaining the fiction of their own "innocence."

What makes most perpetrators especially blameworthy is the fact that they had morally reprehensible motives for trying to sustain their fragile state of ignorance about their own complicity and culpability. They were not passive victims of an evil and overpowering bureaucracy, or innocent and gullible targets of official ideological justifications and propaganda. They actively collaborated, using their own mental powers to the fullest, in order to remain loyal and respectable members of the killing team. Ordinarily, the desire to maintain one's self respect and to avoid guilt feelings is admirable because it is a sign of good character; indeed, a person unconcerned with self-respect would be a sociopath. However, whether a person's desire to maintain a good conscience is really good, overall, depends on how that goal is achieved. When a clear conscience is achieved through a project of self-deceptive evasion of responsibility, it is clearly morally worthless, and the person is actually blameworthy. Self-respect should be based on honest self-assessment, not lies and evasions. The perpetrators had other motives that are transparently bad, such as their selfish concern with their own personal welfare. This included a desire to keep their bureaucratic position, which in most cases would have been relatively safe, comfortable, and secure compared to serving at the front.

Perpetrators also feared (justifiable) punishment by the Allies. By itself, fear is not especially reprehensible, but in fact this fear only gradually replaced what had been one of their dominant motives earlier in the war, what I call feelings of "triumphant nationalism." Most perpetrators, like a large majority of Germans, were extremely patriotic, admired their beloved Fuehrer, Hitler, and fully supported the Nazi regime's policies of aggressive war and conquest during the years from 1939 until 1944 (at least), even if these were at the expense of their European neighbors and cost millions of lives.[42]

They also saw the Final Solution, not as an inhumane atrocity perpetrated on a defenseless and harmless people, but as a necessarily brutal tactic against legitimate racial targets, the Jews. Although for many perpetrators this rationalization was not successful in the long run, it played a major role in enabling them to carry out their duties diligently and efficiently during the most lethal phases of the Final Solution. Thus, although they eventually came to fear punishment by the Allies, for several years they had convinced themselves that their country could do no wrong. Thus, their tremendously misguided patriotism helped motivate their self-deception and contributed to their blameworthiness.

To summarize, Hilberg's explanation why and how bureaucratic perpetrators were able to overcome their moral scruples about participating in the Final Solution refutes the myth of the slippery slope from explanation to exculpation.

B. Franz Stangl: Kommandant of the Death Camps, Sobibor and Treblinka:

The most persuasive evidence that there is no slippery slope from explanation to exculpation comes from the relatively few in-depth studies

---

[42] Jones, *Moral Responsibility*, 163-64.

of individual perpetrators. Gitta Sereny's study of Franz Stangl, *Into That Darkness: An Examination of Conscience*, is especially good.[43] She not only provides a historically accurate narrative of his life as a perpetrator, but because she was interested in his moral responsibility, she also delves deeply into his personality and character. In 1971 Sereny was fortunate enough to have the opportunity to conduct seventy hours of interviews with Stangl shortly before he died in prison where he was serving a life sentence for war crimes. She also interviewed his wife, sister-in-law, daughters, and numerous other people who had known him and worked with him, including fellow perpetrators. As a result, her book provides a great deal of information that is highly relevant for making as assessment of Stangl's blameworthiness for his central role in the Final Solution. Since there is more material in her book than it is possible to present here, I shall restrict my discussion to those aspects of her story that bear on Stangl's heavy reliance on tactics of self-deception.

Franz Stangl was born in Altmuenster, Austria in March 1908 to a family of modest means. According to Stangl, his father, who died when Franz was young, was a strict disciplinarian. Franz left school when he was fifteen to become an apprentice weaver. Less than four years later he had already become a master weaver, an early indication of his high motivation and ambition. He soon realized that there was not much chance of advancement in the weaving trade, so in 1931 he entered basic training at the police academy in Linz. In his interviews with Sereny he recalled that the police training methods were brutal and sadistic, and he remarked specifically on the cynical attitudes toward people that police recruits were expected to adopt.[44]

This is the first evidence Sereny encountered of a striking feature of Stangl's character, namely, his ability to maintain an aloof and detached observer's perspective on activities he found repellent or reprehensible, even when he was himself directly involved in them. From the beginning of his professional career in the police, Stangl's highest priority was to succeed by doing an impeccable job and keeping his nose clean. Moral scruples, personal political opinions, and religious convictions could not be allowed to stand in the way of his professional

---

[43] Sereny, *Darkness*
[44] Sereny, *Darkness*, 28.

duties or jeopardize his advancement. In truth, Stangl never had any strong political or ideological views. This is confirmed by the fact that in 1934 he was sent to CID school for counter-intelligence training, a step that he later called "my first step on the road to catastrophe." After completing his training, he was assigned to ferreting out anti-government activities by a wide range of political opponents of the Austrian regime, whether they were Social Democrats, Communists, or Austrian Nazis. He was truly a non-ideological professional policeman.

Stangl told Sereny that after the German takeover of Austria in 1938, he and a fellow policeman got a well-placed official they knew to add their names to a list of suspected Nazis, because they feared that otherwise they would be under suspicion as unreliable by the new Nazi government and possibly imprisoned in a concentration camp or worse. This bit of political opportunism came back to haunt him during his trial in 1970, when it was used to show that he had been a so-called "illegal Nazi" before the *Anschluss*.[45] However, at the time, the deception was successful, and Stangl had no difficulty remaining with the Austrian police, even after his section was absorbed into the Gestapo in January 1939. Despite the fact that Stangl and his wife were both Catholic, he complied with an order to sign an official document certifying that he was a "believer in God," and that he was prepared to renounce his religion. He told Sereny that he "did not like it," but he did not protest it either. Sereny observes, "signing this document was a decisive step in the gradual process of his corruption," the importance of which was confirmed later by his wife.[46]

As he was drawn deeper and deeper into the Nazi regime's radical policies, Stangl became more and more passive and given to self-deception. Just as he had been repelled by the brutality of his police training, he hated the Germans for their brutality and crudeness, and for the way that they treated his former superiors whom he respected. With hindsight he admitted, "I should have killed myself in 1938 ...That's when it started for me. I must acknowledge my guilt".[47] At the time, however, he had convinced himself that he had no choice but

---

[45] Sereny, *Darkness*, 30-33.
[46] Sereny, *Darkness*, 37.
[47] Sereny, *Darkness*, 39.

to go along with whatever his superiors demanded of him. During his interviews with Sereny, he insisted repeatedly that uncooperative or "unreliable" Austrian police were being shot right and left, and that he feared for his life. Although his fear was not completely unfounded, it seems to have been out of proportion to the actual level of danger he faced, and very likely the result of his own biased assessment of his options. Sereny notes a pattern of self-deception by which Stangl often exaggerated the risks involved in trying to do anything to get himself out of the increasingly horrendous situations in which found himself. He was unable to assert himself, whether it was requesting permission to refuse an assignment to a death camp or applying for a transfer to other duty.

Stangl's involvement in the Final Solution grew out of his assignment in 1940 to the so-called euthanasia program that had been authorized by Hitler in 1939. This secret killing program was justified by tenets of Nazi ideology and was officially supposed to be directed at the elimination of a wide variety of people who were considered to be "useless mouths" being kept alive for no good reason. The officially intended victims were not Jews, but "Aryan" Germans; they included people who were mentally ill, mentally retarded, handicapped, syphilitic, epileptic, and so on. In fact, the program expanded to include other categories of people such as political prisoners. A direct precursor to the Final Solution, its goal was genocidal in nature, and its methods (such as killing with gas), as well as many of its personnel (Stangl among them), were transferred to the killing centers of the Final Solution in Poland. Stangl worked primarily at Hartheim, one of the euthanasia killing centers in Austria, from November 1940 until April 1942. His duties were primarily to ensure that the "eligibility" certificates for people being killed were correct and legally valid. He did not directly take part in the killing; in fact, he did not even see the victims.

Sereny questioned Stangl explicitly about his decision to accept the euthanasia assignment, because she knew that he must have had strong reasons to want to refuse. Mercy killing is forbidden by the Catholic Church, and Stangl's wife was a very devout Catholic; in addition, Stangl had strongly resented being required to renounce his Catholicism a couple of years earlier. According to Stangl, he tried to turn the assignment down on the ground that he was not "well suited" for it, but the official in charge (who was ostensibly sympathetic) persuaded him to accept it anyway by both cajoling him with comforting rationalizations for the killings and with thinly veiled warnings of likely retaliation by Stangl's immediate superior in Linz, a German named Prohaska. Prohaska had already begun disciplinary action against Stangl earlier for having arrested a Nazi party member. Stangl relented and accepted the assignment. Sereny provides Stangl's summary of the reasons that determined his decision:

> The combination of things did; the way he presented it; it was already being done by law in America and Russia; the fact that doctors and nurses were involved; the careful examination of the patients; the concern for the feelings of the population. And then, it is true, for months I had felt myself to be in the greatest danger in Linz from Prohaska. After all, I already knew since March 13, 1938, that it was simpler to be dead in Germany than anywhere else. I was just so glad to get away from Linz.[48]

Stangl's self-deceptive evasion of his responsibility for accepting the assignment emerges in his summary: (1) he justified overriding whatever religious or moral scruples he had against killing the disabled by specious rationalizations, (2) in his mind the mere possibility that some disciplinary action might be taken against him was transformed into his being "in the greatest danger", and (3), so as to leave no room for doubt, he repeated his belief that, in fact, he could have been murdered. It seems most likely that whatever scruples he had against participating in the killing were relatively weak, and that he was much more concerned about his own welfare, including safeguarding his professional career in the police, together with concern for being able to take care of his wife and family. His fear of being murdered was clearly exaggerated and due in large part to self-deception.

Stangl's descent into the hell of the Final Solution came when he was transferred to the extermination center at Sobibor in Poland in April 1942. He served there as *Kommandant* until September and was then transferred to Treblinka where he served as *Kommandant* until that death camp was closed in September 1943. Sereny notes that euthanasia

---

[48] Sereny, *Darkness*, 52.

personnel did not have to go the death camps in Poland; they had some choice. However, she admits to having some doubts about Stangl's claim that he did not know the actual purpose of Sobibor until he actually arrived there. He insisted to her that even when he met for three hours with Lieutenant-General Odilo Globocnik, who was in charge of the extermination camps in Poland, he was kept in the dark. She admits that it is possible that new personnel like Stangl were kept ignorant until they arrived so that they would not have any chance to ask to be relieved until after they were implicated by their knowledge.[49] I shall assume that Stangl's account is the truth; he did not know that he would be in charge of a killing center until he arrived at Sobibor.

When Stangl arrived at Sobibor in April it was not yet operational, and routine killing did not begin until early May 1942. By all accounts, Stangl was an extraordinarily efficient and successful *Kommandant*. He visited the death camp at Belzec, observed how it operated, noted improvements that would be needed, and on his return to Sobibor made sure that the new installation would by more lethally effective.[50] Later at Treblinka, he was responsible for additional "improvements," for example, he stopped using a new group of Jewish workers from each arriving death train to unload the passengers and their baggage and then sending the workers to the gas chambers, too. Instead, a more or less permanent Jewish work *kommando* was kept alive to unload all the trains.[51] He did not make these changes for any humanitarian reasons, but for efficiency. In December 1942, Stangl was assimilated into the SS. By May 1943 his exemplary service was recognized by a promotion to Captain (*Hauptsturmfuehrer*), with a commendation by Globocnik stating, "Stangl is the best camp commander and had the most prominent part in the whole action".[52]

This pattern of conscientiousness and efficiency in carrying out his extermination duties was complemented by Stangl's indifference to the suffering of Jewish victims. In the spring of 1942 a Jewish woman from a nearby village came to Sobibor looking for her husband who had been brought there on a death train. Not realizing what went on in Sobibor

---

[49] Sereny, *Darkness*, 106.
[50] Yitzhak Arad, *Belzec, Sobibor, Treblinka: The Operation Reinhard Death Camps* (Bloomington and Indianapolis: Indiana University Press, 1987), 75, 79-80.
[51] Arad, *Belzec, Sobibor, Treblinka*, 105-06.
[52] Arad, *Belzec, Sobibor, Treblinka*, 168.

and that her husband had already been killed in a gas chamber, she was brought to Stangl. When she asked to visit with her husband, Stangl called in an SS man and signaled that she should be taken out and shot. Later, when he learned that the SS man had not shot the woman himself, but had directed a Ukrainian guard to do it instead, Stangl was furious and called him a coward.[53] Stangl's outlook on his work was completely non-ideological and focused on the practical aims of efficiency and successful results. During an interview, Sereny asked him, "What did you think at the time was the reason for the extermination of the Jew?" Stangl answered, "They wanted their money...Have you any idea of the fantastic sums that were involved? That's how that steel was bought, in Sweden." She then asked, "Why, if they were going to be killed anyway, what was the point of all the humiliation, why the cruelty?" Stangl answered, "To condition those who actually had to carry out the policies ...To make it possible for them to do what they did."[54]

At Treblinka he remained in the background while his subordinates were left free to humiliate, torture, flog, or kill so-called work-Jews.[55] Yet years later, in an interview with Sereny, Stangl claimed that in fact he had had "quite friendly relations" with work-Jews at Treblinka and used an anecdote to prove it. It seems that Stangl had befriended a Jew named Blau and his wife when they arrived on a death train because he had known them from before the war. (Indeed, Sereny makes clear that she detected no evidence at all during her interviews that Stangl was antisemitic.) He arranged good jobs for both of them. What Stangl singled out to illustrate his friendship with Blau, however, was the fact that when Blau's eighty-year-old father arrived on a death train, he granted Blau's request to give his father a meal in the camp kitchen before having him shot in the *Lazarett* (a small building reserved for executions by pistol shot), instead of being killed with everyone else in a gas chamber. According to Stangl, when Blau came to him after it was all over and thanked him, "I said, 'Well, Blau, there's no need to thank me, but of course if you *want* to thank me, you may.'"[56]

---

[53] Arad, *Belzec, Sobibor, Treblinka*, 80.
[54] Sereny, *Darkness*, 101.
[55] Arad, *Belzec, Sobibor, Treblinka*, 199-203.
[56] Sereny, *Darkness*, 207-08.

Explanation, Understanding, and Holding Holocaust Perpetrators Responsible

This incident shows how distorted Stangl's moral judgment had become as the result of continuous self-deception and rationalization while he was *Kommandant* at Treblinka. Also, the fact that he would tell Sereny this story years later in order to lessen his blameworthiness proves how potent self-deception can sometimes be. Of course, it is possible that he no longer believed that he really should get credit for doing "good deeds" for work-Jews, and that he only told the story to Sereny to save face. Even then, his assumption that Sereny would think that his bizarre example reflected well on his character is itself evidence that he had long ago lost all ability to appreciate the horrendous evil of his participation in the Final Solution.

There is a wealth of relevant information in Sereny's account of her interviews with Stangl that I do not have space to include, however, I believe that the material I have presented is sufficient to enable me to make a reasonably justified assessment of Franz Stangl's conduct and character during his participation in the Final Solution. I take for granted that what Stangl did, namely serving as *Kommandant* in Sobibor and Treblinka, was morally wrong. The question I want to answer is to what degree Stangl was blameworthy (morally responsible) for what he did. Ideally, one would prefer to consider each of the four conditions required for full blameworthiness separately. That is, one would ask, in turn, whether Stangl "acted" intentionally, knowingly, voluntarily, and with bad motives. However, Stangl's participation in the Final Solution was not a single, discrete action, but a course of actions engaged in over several years. Moreover, he did not start out knowing that he would end up being in charge of death camps, and he certainly did not intentionally set out to occupy such an important position in the killing process. Instead, his involvement in the Final Solution developed gradually and the degree to which he had to compromise himself increased incrementally, thus, making it easier for him to rationalize each step he took further down the path to genocide. This incremental process was in fact quite insidious, because it meant that he was becoming further and further implicated by his continued participation, yet at each choice point he did not have either the courage or practical wisdom to extricate himself. The fact that Stangl went through this gradual process of self-entrapment, at the beginning of which he did not have either full knowledge of what was to come, or any intention of doing what he ended up doing, is to my mind a significant mitigating factor. However, as I will now try to show, it does not even come close to excusing him altogether.

Stangl is a paradigm of the type of perpetrator who was basically apolitical, neither a Nazi nor an antisemite, who, nevertheless, became a conscientious and dedicated perpetrator of genocide, coldly indifferent to the suffering of the victims. His main goals were to be a respected professional policeman and to provide for and protect his wife and family. He seems to have had at best only weak moral and religious scruples against participating in the Final Solution, since he was able to overcome them and do his job so well that he was promoted and given a glowing commendation. He did not do his job perfunctorily, but with determination and zeal, finding new ways to make the killing system more efficient.

Let us turn now to the questions: What did he know and when did he know it? With respect to the euthanasia program, he knew before he accepted the assignment that it involved killing handicapped patients. However, he overcame his reluctance to accept the assignment by self-deceptive rationalizations and biased assessment of the risks involved if he refused. After that, it was fairly easy for him to avoid confronting the full reality of what his work involved, since he did not have any contact with the victims or take part in the killing. What did he know about the purpose of the camps at Sobibor and Treblinka, and when did he know it? I have already indicated that I am inclined to think that Stangl was telling the truth when he said he knew nothing about the purpose of Sobibor until he arrived there. Consequently, he is relatively blameless for his initial acceptance of that position. However, after he realized that Sobibor was a death camp, he not only did not make any serious effort to get a transfer, but he applied himself more diligently to his duties as *Kommandant*. There is no evidence that he tried to alleviate the plight of the victims or the work-Jews at Sobibor. He certainly knew the purpose of Treblinka before he was transferred there. As we have seen, he was an even more diligent and successful *Kommandant* there. When his wife came to visit him at Treblinka, she tried desperately to convince him to get a transfer, but to no avail.[57]

---

[57] Sereny, *Darkness*, 234-35.

Once he knew the purpose of these death camps, of course, Stangl was intentionally participating in what he knew, or should have known, was immoral. However, the fact that he acted intentionally does not guarantee that he was also doing so voluntarily. Did Stangl in fact have a choice whether to participate or not? Stangl was convinced that he did not. As we will see, there is ample evidence that he did have a choice, so the explanation why he thought otherwise must lie, at least in part, in his extraordinary capacity for self-deception. For example, if he had any moral qualms at all about what he was doing, he was able to stifle them completely. In addition, he was able to convince himself that he had no real choice, and that any attempt to get a transfer would put him and his family in great danger: He would be shot or put in a concentration camp, and his family would be sent to a camp for "unreliables."[58]

At some points in his interviews with Sereny, Stangl was able to admit his tendency to engage in self-deception. For example, he argued that he was not committing a legally punishable offense unless he did something intentionally. And, since he did not have "free will" to disobey, he could not have the requisite intent. When Sereny objected that she did not see how this applied to his situation, he replied," That's what I'm trying to explain to you; the only [way I] could live was by compartmentalizing my thinking. By doing this I *could* apply it to my own situation...."[59]

Was Stangl under coercion? Historians are generally skeptical of this excuse. Earlier, we saw that Hilberg cites examples of perpetrators who disobeyed orders, even in Jewish affairs, and nothing happened to them. Studies of the SS and police battalions have shown that this was a fairly common occurrence.[60] Christopher Browning, summed up the consensus of most historians:

> Quite simply, in the past forty-five years, no defense
> attorney or defendant in any of the hundreds of postwar
> trials has been able to document a single case in which

---

[58] Sereny, *Darkness*, 235.
[59] Sereny, *Darkness*, 164.
[60] Ernst Klee, Willi Dressen, and Volker Riess, *The Good Old Days: The Holocaust as Seen by Its Perpetrators and Bystanders* (New York: The Free Press, 1988), 76-86.

refusal to obey an order to kill unarmed civilians resulted
in the allegedly dire punishment.[61]

It seems reasonable to conclude that Stangl was self-deceived about
not having a choice. Moreover, his resulting ignorance was culpable, because
it resulted primarily from his motivated project of evading his guilt for
continuing his participation in the killing when he really did not have to.

Finally, we can ask: What were his primary motives for engaging in
self-deception and how did these reflect on his character? Although he did
have some moral and religious scruples about participating in the Final
Solution, he seems to have been mostly motivated by fear and professional
ambition. His deathly fear of punishment was not realistically based and it
betrayed an inordinate preoccupation with his own well-being. At the same
time, he was an exacting *Kommandant* who wanted not merely to stay out
of trouble, but to do an outstanding job. In the process, he made the killing
machine even more efficient and deadly than it might have been otherwise.
While his concern to care for his wife and family were understandable and
justified, his primary motives were unworthy and reflect badly on his
character. We know that he lied to his wife about almost every aspect of his
involvement in the killing of the Jews.[62] He was only secondarily concerned
to quiet his conscience about what he was doing. If anything, he became
hardened and indifferent to the suffering of the Jewish victims.

My overall conclusion is that Franz Stangl was to a very high degree
blameworthy for his participation in the Final Solution. Of course, this
assessment is based on my interpretation of material drawn from Sereny's
study; others will surely interpret her book differently. In addition, new
research may uncover information that sheds a different light on Stangl's
career and character. Whatever the outcome of further research may be, I
think I have confirmed my basic thesis that explanation does not inevitably
lead to excusing and exoneration. For what it is worth, I should add that
Sereny claims that Stangl in fact explicitly admitted his guilt to her in the
last interview she had with him. She thinks it is not coincidental that he
died the very next day.[63]

[61] Christopher Browning, *Ordinary Men: Reserve Police Battalion 101 and the Final Solution in Poland* (New York: HarperCollins, 1992), 170.
[62] Sereny, *Darkness*, 337-67.
[63] Sereny, *Darkness*, 364-66.

Those Left Behind
Rene Firestone

The Judgment of Herbert Bierhoff attempts to pack the entire Holocaust into one neat package, dealing with too many issues both during and after the Holocaust, and layering story over story. I will address only two of the major stories, both having to do with faith and morality in the concentration camps.

The most important story in the play has to do with Herbert killing his own daughter, Ellen, because he has information that the next day all the children in the ghetto will be taken away. What the reader has to deal with is how to put Herbert's soul to rest after his death, and how to help Shimon, Ellen's friend and confidant, find peace in life.

After fifty years, Shimon asks survivor friends to pass judgment on Herbert Bierhoff's soul. This is not a fair request. In spite of the survivor's suffering, how would they know what it is to die a humiliating, violent death at the hands of the Nazis? Only those who suffered such death could judge Herbert for saving his child from that fate.

The question is: Can there be any doubt that Herbert acted out of pure love when he poisoned Ellen? The survivors argue whether Herbert knew for sure that Ellen would suffer a violent death. Of course, this question cannot be answered. But, given the fact that Herbert was a Jewish policeman in Riga, it is probable that he truly believed it. He was willing to suffer the consequences alone to save his child from the terror of the Nazis. He didn't even tell his wife about it because he didn't want her to be involved or feel responsible in any way. Abraham also did not tell Sarah according to the Rabbinic commentaries on the *Akeidah*. The consequences of his actions, however, depend on whether he believed or trusted God. If Herbert believed that he was entrusting Ellen to God instead of letting the Nazis take her, then, of course, he believed in and trusted God, and only did the same as Abraham was willing to do to please God. But, God stopped Abraham and saved his son. It seems that, in Riga, even God could not save Ellen from the evil of mankind. Therefore, God must forgive Herbert and put his soul to rest.

At one point, Herbert's wife, Ruth, comforts him, saying that God will forgive him for witnessing the liquidation of the older prisoners. His answer to her is, "Should I forgive God?" Either way, he acknowledges God's existence.

It is interesting that so many survivors, including Shimon's friends, claim that they don't believe in God after the Holocaust. I think that those survivors would rather deny God than question Him, accuse Him, or argue with Him. Does that mean that they fear God? And if they do, doesn't that confirm their belief in God?

The question remains how to deal with these issues morally. Those of us who experienced the *Shoah* know that the morality by which we live is not the same morality that applied in the camp. For example, a mother arrives to Auschwitz with three children, one in her arm, two others hanging onto her skirt. She comes in front of Doctor Mengele— the "Angel of Death"— who informs her that she can take only one child with her; the others must go to the other side. She must now choose which child stays with her and which will go. These are what we survivors refer to as "choiceless choices." How can a mother morally justify choosing one child in place of another, even though she doesn't know who will be saved or who will be killed.

In our barrack, the *Kapo* [overseer] found a pregnant woman. She didn't know what to do with her. If she reports it to the Nazi Commander, the mother and baby will both be killed, so she decides to save the mother, but the baby must die. Was saving the mother a moral judgment? As a survivor, fifty some years after the Holocaust, how could I pass judgment on anyone who was killed in the *Shoah*?

Later in the story, Shimon asked his friends to tell him what would they have done in Herbert's place. The question becomes, "How can someone who doesn't believe in God make any kind of a moral judgment about anything? After all, aren't God's Ten Commandments the basis of all morality?" The survivors also talked about the devil or Satan's role in the camps. Were they talking about a Godly Satan or a human Satan? Then one of them remarked that when Satan pushed too far, Herbert acted, while they did nothing.

Another survivor said, "We are the 'living dead' since the *Shoah*." Shimon's dilemma may be expressed in this remark. The survivors in the story did not learn from their experiences, they still are preoccupied with death, not life; with the past, not with the future. They are still embarrassed by their experiences. I wonder why we feel so differently about the tragic past we shared.

Today, I feel great pride in being a Jew. For whatever reason, my life was spared. I understand that I have a responsibility to future generations.

I also know that, by dealing with the Holocaust and speaking about my experiences, I give voice to those we so tragically left behind.

Interview with Dr. Sigi Ziering
Rene Firestone

Interview With Dr. Sigi Ziering

An Interview with Dr. Sigi Ziering—February 28, 1999
Rene Firestone Interviewer, Survivors of the Shoah Visual History Foundation

Good morning Mr. Ziering... Where were you born and when?

I was born on March 20, 1928 in Kassel, Germany.

Where did you grow up?

Until 1941, I lived in Kassel.

What do your friends call you?

Sigi.

Tell us about your father.

My father's first name was Isaac, and he was a merchant.

© Survivors of the Shoah Visual History Foundation, 1999. All rights reserved. Reprinted with permission.

Your relationship with him?

It was a very good relationship.

What do you remember most?

I guess I remember his generosity and his leadership in the community. We were Polish Jews living in Germany, and he was the head of the Polish Jewish organization in Kassel. We had our own small synagogue and he provided that leadership.

What was your personal relationship with him? Did you travel with him?

That was rather difficult. It required a lot of traveling, and since 1933 or '34 it was rather difficult for Jews to travel, so it wasn't a good idea to tag along.

Your Mother?

Cilly. She, too, came from Poland. She provided a very warm and comforting home.

Any favorite stories about her?

I think the reason I'm alive today was partly because of her efforts during the camp days, and luckily she's still alive...At one period, my brother and I were in a concentration camp in Latvia called Kaiserwald and she was in a less severe camp run by the army clothing depot. She virtually threw herself at the commanding officer of that camp and begged him to get us transferred from Kaiserwald to the army clothing depot. For some reason, he listened to her and did.

Your siblings?

One brother, still alive.

Interview With Dr. Sigi Ziering

What was your relationship like as children?

My brother is one year older. His name is Herman. We had a very close relationship, obviously a rivalry between siblings, but outside of this we got along very well. He protected me and I looked after him.

Can you tell us a little about your family's religious identity?

We were observant Jews, I guess more so at my mother's behest than my fathers. He was quite religious himself, but we kept the holidays. We did not strictly observe *Shabbas*. We kept a kosher home.

Did you go to religious school?

When I started school, it was no longer possible to go to a secular school, so we had to go to a Jewish community school.

Were you observant?

To a certain degree, yes.

Did you think that was different, that you couldn't go to public school?

It's not that I missed it, but it sort of set us apart.

Did you ever have non-Jewish school?

Not as far as I can remember. You're talking about the childhood?

Yes. Do you recall your parents having non-Jewish friends?

Maybe they were friendly with one or two families who were non-Jewish, yes.

As a child, did you notice a difference between the Jewish and non-Jewish communities?

They were friends, but they were not very intimate friends that you would see once or twice a week, so it's hard to judge whether they acted differently than other casual friends.

Were teachers Jewish?

Yes.

Did they tell you things about things changing in the country?

Not as far as I can remember.

Did you know that there were changes in the country?

Of course. There were certain restrictions on Jews, things they could do or couldn't do. They ended up wearing the Star of David. We couldn't go to swimming clubs; we couldn't go to movies after a certain time. We were subject to ridicule, to being beaten up by the Hitler youths. We knew that something was going on.

How old were you when it started?

I think it started drastically after *Kristallnacht,* which was 1938, at which point I was 10 years old. But to a certain degree you knew it before that, because of people being picked up and sent to Dachau or Buchenwald or other places, friends of the family who never returned. People tried to emigrate. Store windows were damaged, or SS marched around and prevented people from going to Jewish stores.

As a child, what did you think about those things? What did it mean to you?

You knew you were different. I guess you sort of wondered if the strangeness was your making or somebody else's making. I don't know.

I'd like to pursue this feeling of "is it of our making"? Why did it even enter the mind?

Well, a constant barrage: Hitler's speeches, the newspapers, the taunts of the non-Jewish children, being attacked by the Hitler youths and not being able to defend yourself, having to run and to run. I guess it had an impression at 8 years…maybe they're right. Maybe you're part of this hated race. Maybe you're different.

Did you confront your parents with these thoughts?

No.

You mentioned Kristallnacht. How do you remember it?

I remember rather well because our store windows were smashed. The main synagogue went up in flames. My father managed to go in and rescue a Sefer Torah which is now in a museum in Brooklyn. Most of our friends were taken to Buchenwald. My father went into hiding so he was not caught. To say the least, it was a noisy night and we all feared for our safety.

Were any of your close friends or family involved?

Yes. Quite a few of my friend's fathers were taken.

Did you notice a difference between how people treated you?

There was definitely a hesitation of people to, even those who wanted to be friendly, to be identified with being friendly or talking to Jews.

What did your teachers tell you?

They didn't tell us anything.

When did you personally realize that the family was in danger?

I guess we never realized it…Our parents tried to shield us from what happened in Buchenwald and Dachau, though once in a while you'd get these death notices and knew something was definitely wrong. But there wasn't much discussion in front of us by our parents telling us what the dangers were, though we could overhear them once in a while.

How did you children deal with it?

I don't know. I guess you just accepted it.

When World War II started, did anything change?

When it started, my father was no longer there. He had left for England a few months earlier. There was a general euphoria as the Germans celebrated victory after victory marching through Poland and into all the other countries that they conquered.

Did you think it would affect your life?

Well school started for us, and we felt more isolated than ever, but I guess also not being able to communicate with my father was difficult. But we were still optimistic. We couldn't imagine things could get much worse.

How did you find out you could no longer go to school.

We were just told that at such and such a date it would close.

You stayed in Germany how long?

We stayed in Germany until December 1941. In December 1941, a thousand of us were asked to assemble in a sports hall of a local gymnasium and to bring 50 pounds or 50 kilos, I don't remember, of personal belongings. We reported there the night before and were asked to register and leave all our valuables and so on...20 or 30 Deutschmarks each. We slept there overnight and the next morning they marched us to the main railroad station in Kassel, boarded a train, and four days later we arrived in Riga, Latvia.[1]

---

[1] The deportation of Jews from Kassel to Riga was part of the Nisko plan, which envisioned ridding the Reich of its Jews by shipping them to conquered areas in the East. This plan was never fully adopted and was superceded by the "Final Solution," the murder of European Jews.

Interview With Dr. Sigi Ziering

Before you went to the station, what did you think was going to happen?

We were told that we would be resettled in the East—we weren't told anything specifically, but that they had work for us in the East and we would be resettled there.

Was your grandmother still with you?

No, she had left before the war for Poland.

How did your mother feel with the two boys?

I think she saw hard times ahead. I think she expected severe hardships. But I don't think she expected anything of the hardships we experienced.

When you got to the railroad station, you boarded what kind of trains?

We were sort of lucky; they were regular 3rd class passenger trains. Not open boxcars like some other people.

How long did the journey last?

Four days.

Can you describe those four days?

I guess for the children it was exciting. Looking out the windows. We went through Poland, we went through Lithuania, we went through a big part of Germany and ended up in Latvia. Exploring the train, running around and so on. For the older people it must have been very uncertain, not knowing what to expect.

About your mother…how did she react?

Normally, in these situations, she would present her best face to us and be upbeat.

Did the children just behave like children in general?

Absolutely.

The train arrived where?

In a suburb or Riga. Not in the main railroad station - it was a freight station outside of Riga where we unloaded. It was bitter cold. There was snow and ice on the ground. We were greeted by SS, with guns and dogs. We were immediately asked to disembark and leave our luggage. We were asked to line up. We were greeted by Oberstürmbannführer Kauser, who was the commandant of the Riga ghetto and the first selection started. We didn't know what was going on except that some of the men were asked to move over to the right or left. It turns out later that most of the men were sent to Salispils, which was a sub-camp of the Riga ghetto. And then the rest of us were sent to the ghetto.

You remained with your mother and brother?

The three of us remained together, yes. There was one incident during the march where somebody tried to put a letter in a mailbox on the way to the ghetto and was shot.

What did you think?

I didn't know what to think.

Which month was this?

December 1941.

How long did you stay in the ghetto?

Until about the summer of 1943.

What was it like there?

Well, when we entered the ghetto, and this we found out later, it was a ghetto that had been previously occupied by about 35,000 Latvian Jews, and just a week before we arrived, approximately 30,000 of these Latvian Jews were marched into the forest and killed in mass graves. So when we arrived in the ghetto a week later, there was evidence of plundering, evidence of a rapid evacuation, food still on the table, in some cases you saw blood spots either in the snow or outside so we knew that something drastic had happened. As it is, they kept about four or five thousand Latvian men and separated them within part of the ghetto. We weren't supposed to talk to them but we talked to them and found out what happened.

Did you work in the ghetto?

My mother worked in the ghetto, yes. Shoveling the snow, cleaning the streets, cutting down wood....

What did the children do?

After the initial few weeks, they established a school. We went to school for a few months and then the selections started and my mother wisely decided that we would be safer in a working commando, those who volunteered to work and go out of the ghetto, during the day at least.

Who organized the school?

The ghetto internally was run by Jewish Council.

I'd like to go back to the transport just before Riga. Was there any Jewish leadership in Germany?

There was Jewish leadership, but it was very ineffective. It was basically taking orders from the Gestapo and carrying them out.

And did they inform you of what's going on, where you're going to go, what to expect?

No. I think all the [unintelligible] was to report to the gymnasium in a few days and bring specified amounts of clothing.

Did the leadership go with you?

It wasn't a complete transport from Kassel. I think there was a total of 2,500 Jews in Kassel and the surroundings, and we were the first transport. I think, most likely, though I don't know for a fact, the leadership did not go with them.

What work did you do in the ghetto?

All sorts of work. I worked in the cement factory. I shoveled snow, cleaning the streets of snow in the wintertime. I helped unload ships. I cleaned the streets occasionally.

Did you have any contact with the Latvians?

Oh yes. The contact with the Latvians was for me a little difficult because I didn't speak Latvian or Russian, but some of them did speak German. The Latvians were no better or worse than the Germans, at least in my opinon. There were some who treated us very sympathetically and others who treated us like scum.

How was the food situation?

Pretty bad. We got the minimum rations in the ghetto after the first four weeks. We didn't get anything for the first four weeks. But after you went out to work you either traded clothing—we had a polite term for stealing called organizing. Organize some food, did various things.

Did the Latvians outside help you?

They helped us in the sense of being trade partners, I don't think they overtly tried to help us. Some did, a few did.

Interview With Dr. Sigi Ziering

How long did you stay in Riga?

Actually I stayed in Riga until 1944, but in the ghetto until the summer of 1943.

Why?

At that time, the Russians were moving closer and already had thrown the Germans back, and were beginning to get into Poland. So actually there was a whole army group stretching from Leningrad to Lithuania in the Baltic section that was sort of being isolated. When that happened the Germans decided to close down the ghetto and at that time they had started a concentration camp called Kaiserwald not far from Riga, and some of us ended up there.

Were you the first prisoners in Kaiserwald?

No. I came there in the summer of 1943 and it was an established camp at that time.

What was the life like in Kaiserwald?

Kaiserwald was pretty brutal, starting with the morning appeals, the standing out for one two or three hours every morning. 'Mitz up, Mitz down. Head up, head down. Cap up, cap down.' Exercise and shenanigans like that. A minimum of food. Outside work in quarries. Things like that. We carried bricks from one place to the other. The next day you'd bring them back to the first place. Killings and beatings...

You mentioned the commander, Krauser. Did he go with you to Kaiserwald?

No. I heard that he was transferred to fighting partisans and apparently lost his life. Kaiserwald was run by Kommandant Sauer.

And what was he like?

Animal.

Tell us a little bit about Kaiserwald. Describe a day. When did you get up? When were you fed?

We got up at, I don't remember, 5 or 6 in the morning, and you would have to be out of the barracks and go over to the washroom, some toilet facilities—well, toilet facilities were actually a latrine in a separate building. You had a few moments to wash yourself with cold water and back to the barracks and get dressed. Then the count started and you were sorted into working commandos, marched out of the camp, worked 'til noon and maybe got some soup. Worked again 'til 5 or 6 and marched back.

Did you stay in the same barracks as your mother?

My mother wasn't in Kaiserwald. She was directly transferred to this army clothing camp, Muehlgraben, a suburb of Riga.

You were separated from you family when?

I was the first one of our family to end up in Kaiserwald. My brother came three months later when they finally dissolved the ghetto, and at that time my mother was transferred to the clothing camp.

Did you know that you were going to be reunited, or what were your thoughts?

No. We had no idea. I had no contact. My mother claimed later she was once on the truck and saw a group of us marching on the street and she thought she recognized me from the truck.

What went through your head when you were finally separated from both of them? How old were you?

I was 15. I don't think you thought about it too much because you tried not to think about it. You tried to...your main thoughts were, 'Where's the next piece of bread coming from, where do I get the one piece of clothing to protect me from the cold, or how do I not get a beating at night?'

Did you think about your father?

Infrequently. If I thought about him I thought that he was lucky to get to England and also because of his nature and, shouldn't say aggressive, but not being a person who takes things lightly, I don't think he would have lasted long in the ghetto or the camps.

How long did you stay in Kaiserwald?

About 4 ½ months.

And then you went where?

That's what I referred to initially when my mother, knowing that both of us were in Kaiserwald, threw herself at the feet of the Wehrmacht officer in control of this clothing depot and he managed to get the two of transferred out of Kaiserwald into the army clothing depot.

Where was it?

Muehlgraben

Was it a camp?

It was run by the army. It was a camp, we had barbed wire, we had guards, but these were all army personnel so the naked brutality of the SS wasn't there and things were a little better.

By this time, did you know any places called extermination camps?

Well, we knew that, as I mentioned before, that 30,000 Latvian Jews had been shot in the forest back in 1941. We knew that whole transports never arrived back at the ghetto because the clothing came a few days later. We knew that all transports ended up in the forests and they were killed. We knew what went on in places like Salisburg, where people were starved to death. As they were in the ghetto, too. It wasn't any revelation to us, but we didn't know about the existence of Auschwitz or places like that.

How long did you stay in the clothing camp?

We stayed until I guess it must have been September or so of 1944...At that time the Russians had finally isolated the German army group in the Baltics and were closing up on Riga, so this particular clothing depot decided to move its operations from Riga to a more western place in Latvia, which was also a port called Libau and therefore they took the Jews that were working in this particular army camp to Libau.

What was Libau like?

Libau was also run by the army. Repairing army clothing that came from the front with bullet holes and blood all over it and reconditioning it so they could reissue it. It wasn't much different from the army camp in Riga because again we had army supervision.

Did you have contact with the soldiers?

Oh yes.

What was the relationship?

That was getting to a time where I guess most, except a few fanatics, realized Germany had lost the war, so it was a little change in tone and attitude, but not too much.

Did you know why the attitude changed?

Well, we had enough contact from what we overheard, and occasionally we picked up papers, and the papers talked about victories and so on. If you read between the lines, you knew if the Russians were in Poland and approaching the German border, and the Allies had landed, that these were not [German] victories. Also, we had frequent attacks by Russian bombers.

How was Libau different from Kaiserwald?

Libau was more like Muehlgraben. It was a camp run by the army, but Kaiserwald was a typical concentration camp.

You stayed in Libau how long?

We stayed in Libau I think until February 1945. And at that time I guess the SS prevailed and felt—I don't know what they felt—but for some reason, they loaded us onto a ship and took us back to Hamburg.

How long did the journey last?

About seven or eight days.

Let me go back to the Latvian camps. How were you transported from one to another?

From Riga to Libau we went by ship. From the ghetto to Kaiserwald I guess we marched by foot.

This was in the months of December. Did you have sufficient clothing?

Absolutely not. [Laughs.]

So you are leaving for Hamburg now. This is when?

This must have been either February or early March of 1945.

Did you know how the war was progressing?

Oh, yes. When we entered the Hamburg harbor you could see the destruction, the terrible destruction of Hamburg. Also, on the ship, we talked more openly to the sailors, who were less [mean] than the other segment of the German military, and knew it was pretty close to the end.

Do you have any thoughts about returning to Germany at this time and seeing Germany destroyed like that?

I guess probably—the German expression was *schadenfreude*—retribution at the payback that they were getting.

Did you have any feelings of returning home?

By that time I don't think I regarded my home in Germany as anything I wanted to return to.

What were the conditions on the ship?

On the ship we slept on munitions boxes. It was very uncomfortable. It was a rough sea. We could see Sweden from the ship and were hoping that they'd make a mistake and end up in Sweden, but that didn't happen.

You and your brother, did you discuss things?

I guess we discussed many things, but I don't think we speculated as to the outcome because we didn't want to upset each other. What we discussed is how to organize the next piece of cheese or salami or whatever.

How did your mother hold up under these conditions?

We never asked these questions. We just did what we had to do and we did it. I don't think we thought about it or reflected on it.

What happened when you arrived?

We arrived in Hamburg and we were taken to the main police transport, which turns out to be one of the largest prisons in Germany—a regular police prison by the name of Fussbertel.

Interview With Dr. Sigi Ziering

Do you remember the date?

It was probably March of 1945.

You stayed in this prison how long?

Probably six to eight weeks. The SS had a van to transfer people from Fussbertel to Bergen-Belsen. This van could only accommodate 10 or 12 of us at a time, and it would only go to Bergen-Belsen once a week. So at this German prison they decided to do this alphabetically, and obviously we had an advantage because of our last name. So this went on for about a few weeks and then I guess Bergen-Belsen was liberated by the British. [Since] the British were also threatening Hamburg, ...they took us out of Fussbertel and marched us to Kielhesse, a small camp. There were no other Jews in that particular camp. When we arrived, the *kommandant* addressed us and I guess couldn't hide his joy or his surprise because he couldn't believe that Jews were still alive, and he was planning to do something about it. There we started again with the appearance every morning and the beatings, and the thievery of clothing. In this case we carried barracks from one section to another section. And the next day we had to pick them up and run back with them. And whoever couldn't make it was shot. Certain days we also went into Kiel and were asked to clean up debris from bomb damage.

Tell us about the march from the police prison to the camp.

There were 200 of us and I think it lasted about four days. The SS was a Flemish SS contingent and I remember being beaten up by one [of them]. I do remember when we went through a small town that a woman with a child came over and gave somebody some bread. An SS man accosted her, but she really wasn't afraid of him. She yelled at him and told him her husband had been killed and it was inhuman what they were doing. It was sort of an eye-opener to us that someone was talking back to the SS and no longer afraid of them.

Were you fed at all on this journey?

I think we got provisions from the police prison before we left. The police prison in Hamburg was really a vacation of sorts for us because we had straw mattresses and shower facilities and were fed regularly every day, so the provisions we got for the march from Hamburg to Kiel were pretty good.

Who was on this march?

Just 200 or 250 Jews who had come from Libau. Well, some of them had been sent to Bergen-Belsen, so maybe there were 150 of us.

Men and women?

Men and women.

You arrived to Kielhesse and what happened?

Well, as I described, we were greeted by the *kommandant*, who expressed his joy at seeing Jews. He couldn't understand why Jews were still alive. [At the camp] the conditions were pretty brutal. We carried these barrack parts. I remember one night—this takes us to the end of April, 1945, and things were in turmoil. There was a group of 40 to 50 Polish officers who were sort of segregated in that camp and they took them out and shot them. We didn't have much hope left at that time because we were sure that they [the Germans] were going down, but they would take us down with them. And I think this may have been on April 30, at night, and these SS men came into our barrack and told us to prepare to go to Sweden the next day. Since we couldn't go in zebra clothes—we needed civilian clothes—they took us to the morgue and asked us to undress the dead people and bring them back into the barracks so we could change into civilian clothing. I remember one of the morgue victims still showed signs of life so [one Nazi] took out his pistol and shot him. When we came back to the barracks and distributed the clothes, we speculated [that] they probably wanted us in civilian clothes so it wouldn't be too obvious when we were killed.

Next morning, as we got up, [we] were asked to separate from the rest of the camp and aggregate in the main section. Assembled and indeed there were some buses with the red cross sign and flying Swedish flags.

There were a number of kind people with doctors and nurses uniforms and heavily Scandinavian accents who started talking to us. We were still afraid that this might be a trap, but we didn't have much choice anyhow, so we boarded the buses and a couple of hours later we entered Denmark, which was still occupied by the Germans at that time. They took us to a delousing station in Denmark and then they put us on a train to Copenhagen. I remember when we arrived in Copenhagen they still had the German military patrol at the railroad station but the Danes were very excited and milling around our train and telling us that Hitler had died. From there they took us on the ferry to Sweden and the next day, May 1ˢᵗ, we arrived. And that was the end.

When you were in the camp and told to put on civilian clothing, did you have a chance to talk to your mother?

No, the males and females were separated in this camp.

Did you know she would go with you?

I was hoping she would.

You said you doubted this was a real transport. Did you discuss this with your brother?

We all discussed it—all of us—I think we stayed up all night and discussed it. I guess, overall, most of them were pessimistic and thought it was a trap, but I don't remember the details.

What condition were you and your brother in when you arrived in Sweden?

We were undernourished, but we also didn't look so bad mainly because we were full of water. We were one of the later groups of people to come to Sweden. Apparently, they had managed to take some of the people from the other camps like Ravensbrük, and some of the Jews they got special permission to take out of Thereisenstadt. And by the time we arrived they had learned that it wasn't proper for them to give us chocolate and sweets and all the food we wanted, so we ended up in the hospital. They were very careful of how to feed us and how to bring us back to a normal diet.

Was your mother on this transport?

Yes.

When did you find out?

We found out the minute we boarded the busses. We saw that whatever happened, it would be together.

Tell us what happened after you realized you were free?

I think the first few weeks, as far as I can remember, there was [a] sort of numbness. You didn't think, you simply accommodated to the new circumstances. You slept a lot. You didn't really make plans for the future. We knew my father was in England, but we didn't have any address so we contacted the Red Cross. But for some reason, it took about four or five months before they located him.

When you were reunited with your father, did he have any idea what happened to you? What did you say?

Before he came over to Sweden—at that time it was immediately after the war and it was hard to get flight arrangements—I had sent him a letter about three or four pages where I detailed all the places we had been and what had happened. I have a copy of this, and it has all the dates.

Can you describe your reunion?

The reunion was wonderful—it was a little bit difficult because he came over in the fall or winter—I don't remember exactly—and the flight couldn't land in Stockholm, so it landed in Gertawalk. We waited at the airport in Stockholm and, finally, were told that the flight had landed in

Gertawalk and [that] they'd come over the next morning by train. We went home very disappointed. The next morning, we went to the railroad station and recognized him immediately. It was...very joyful.

How did you feel seeing him after so many years, and your father was sort of waiting? Did you want to talk about it?

I guess maybe my mother did but I don't think my father—after he had seen my letter with all the details—talked too much about the details. Occasionally, he would ask what happened to such and such, but our discussions centered mainly on what to do from here.

Did you find out what happened to your grandmother?

We never found out.

So you went to England.

I hadn't been to school except for the first five years of elementary school and I had a desire to get a university education. So I went to a tutorial college in London for about a year, and on the basis of that I was able to matriculate as an external student.

Did you speak English when you got there?

No. I matriculated as an external student. Then, in 1948, I think, I entered the University of London. By that time, my father decided that for our sake it would be better to move to the United States, so in 1949 we immigrated.

How about your brother?

He didn't decide to pick up his education, so he trained as a diamond cleaver.

When did you come to the U.S. and how did you get here?

We came by boat, actually the Queen Mary, in April 1949. After a few months, I enrolled in Brooklyn College to continue my education and worked in a clothing store on weekends and evenings. [I] graduated with a degree in physics in 1953.

What did your father do?

My father was a merchant and he went back into the clothing business.

After college, what then?

After college I immediately went to graduate school in 1953. After I finished Brooklyn College, I went to Syracuse and got both my masters and Ph.D. in physics in 1957. Meanwhile, in 1953, I met Marilyn and we got married.
When did you meet her?

I met her, actually, in the Borschtbelt—the Catskill Mountains in New York.

And why did you move to California?

California came about 12 years later. After I graduated, I went to work in Boston for a company and subsequently started my own company. About 10 years [later], I sold the [business] to a California company, that then brought me out here as a corporate director of research. And so I ended up in California.

Tell us a little bit about how you met your wife?

[Laughs.] I guess she was there for vacation with her parents at this hotel, and my friend and I decided to go up there for a weekend. She was playing ping pong, and I started playing ping pong with her and we're still playing. [Laughs.]

After you got married, did you join a temple?

Uh, no. In Syracuse—this was graduate school—we either went to Hillel services or drove down to New York for the high holidays to spend with our parents or her parents. But once we moved to Boston, we immediately joined a temple, yes.

Your parents, when they came to the U.S., did they immediately go back to observing Judaism?

Oh, yes.

Your first child is born. What goes through your head? What do you feel is important to tell this child?

Um, actually, I don't think I had these reflections at that time. I think the joy was so overpowering I simply didn't ask myself that question—what should be told, what shouldn't be told—that's basically an attitude that prevailed for most of the time.

How important to you was it that this child grows up to be a Jew?

That was very important, but I sort of didn't want to do it on the back of the Holocaust, so to speak.

Do you remember when you talked about it for the first time?

I think it's maybe 20 years ago, during a Passover seder service, I think. I read that letter that I mentioned before when I explained to my father what had happened in the years I didn't see him, and that was the first time we had an open discussion—not much of a discussion. I read the letter and for some reason there wasn't much discussion. I guess, in those years, you didn't really want to bring up the subject. It was sort of taboo. People weren't really interested. I mean, your family might have been, but outside of your family nobody was interested. It was almost like carrying a stigma on your shoulders that a) you survived when others didn't and b) you seemed to be still different even in a free country. I don't know whether that's the guilt that you carry.

Would you mind reading a little bit of that letter that you wrote to your father?

[READING] 'In December of 1941 there were about 34,000 Jews in the Riga ghetto. From these in the period between the 7th and 9th of December, about 29,000 were murdered by Latvian and German SS. When we entered the ghetto, we found signs of blood all over. The murderers were allowed to plunder the ghetto. Ten people were assigned a small room and kitchen. For the first three weeks we did not receive any food at all. Within two months there arrived about 11,000 Jews from Germany, Austria, and Czechoslovakia. Every third day we had roll call in which the able men were selected and sent [away]. There they died of hunger and exposure, vermin and beatings. Another transport from Berlin arrived in January in the ghetto at 42 degrees below zero—75 persons in a cattle car. On the way, 60 [had] died from exposure and the rest had at least one hand or foot frostbitten. All other transports that arrived in Riga after that were immediately taken...where they were gassed or shot. The clothing of these people was brought into the ghetto where the SS had it sorted and sent away to Germany to the WHW, which means Winter Health Works. On April 5, 1942 and April 8, 1942, 2400 elderly people were taken away from the ghetto. They, too, went the way of the four million. In the beginning of March, the first working groups left the ghetto. Altogether, from about 13,000 Jews in the ghetto, about 9,000 went to work daily. Most of the work was for the army, SS, railway, and mail. Most of the people employed outside of the ghetto were able to trade or get access to an additional piece of bread and thus the food situation in the ghetto was a little bit better. The official food ration per day in the ghetto was 200 grams of bread, which was almost inedible, 5 grams of barley, 3 grams of fat and, from time to time, [some] stinking potatoes.'

I would like you to read the ending also. How many pages was this?

It's about nine pages...[READS] 'At six p.m. we left and we arrived on May 2, 1945, in Copenhagen. The same evening we went on the ferry that took us to Marmay, Sweden. A rabbi greeted us with *Shalom* and "We're not in *prisonfreud*." The four years were not in vain and free Jews still existed in Europe. Again, the same night, we were deloused and received new clothing from head to toe. Seeing Mutti in the bus, I hardly recognized her. And then traveling through Marmay, a city without any damages, full of light at 2 a.m. For heaven's sake, if planes should come now. And finally a real bed covered in white linen. How long has it been? Four years? Are these beds for Jews? Concentration camp inmate 3913? Is this a mistake? Does the Gestapo not exist anymore? No SS, no SD? And then the Swedish people. Does there exist any better? We're allowed to sing the "Hatikvah," listen to the radio, read newspapers, write letters, and what couldn't we do? And, finally, peace, capitulation, no more Nazis, not for nothing 4 million victims. Does justice exist after all?...Remain a thousand times greeted and kissed. Yours, Sigi.'

Is there anything else you want to say?

Well, the only thing is, I mentioned it before, my mother lives in the back here and she is close to 98 this year. She sort of has at last forgotten about the Holocaust as she gets older—for the last 10 or 20 years it had been an obsession with her. She listens to newscasts and sees there's a fire and immediately connects that fire to another Holocaust or to the wellbeing of her family, and it's tremendously upsetting to see her in her waning years to still be totally occupied with the Holocaust and the protection of the family.

Does she talk to the grandchildren about it?

She used to talk about it, but lately she's very confused.

What is your opinion about the state of the world as far as learning the Holocaust?

Well, there seems to be a change in emphasis or attitude. Movies like *Shoah* or *Schindler's List*, especially in the last 10 years seem to have— and the museum of course in Washington and elsewhere—seem to have reawakened an interest in the Holocaust and trying to find out [the] why and how and what the lessons are. I don't know what the lessons are.

What is your message or your legacy to your grandchildren and future generations?

A very difficult question. I sometime think there is no message, there is no lesson, because ultimately it simply shows how inhuman people can be to other people, and for whatever reason, not to the same degree, it seems to repeat itself in Laos and Kosovo right now, in various African nations—Rwanda, and so on. I'm still debating whether—of course you should talk about it—you should remind people of it, you should be objective about it. But whether it will do any good, I don't know.

A Tribute to My Father
at the Inaugural Event for the
Sigi Ziering Institute
University of Judaism

October 2002

Roseanne Ziering

A Tribute to My Father

I am named after my father's cousin, Judith, who perished under the Nazi's at the age of four. My father and his family hid her in the ghetto for two years before she was found and taken away during a selection. I know my father adored this little girl. I know this partly from what he said to me, but more so from what he didn't say. Daddy spoke little but said much. Afraid to burden his children, but also compelled to somehow make us understand his experience, my father lived with this survivor conundrum. All the awful mysteries of life were revealed to the survivors, and it was in this quiet place—where words were just too average—that my father lived. I know the young boy that was my father wanted to save his cousin and was helpless to do so. I know he felt he failed her. I understood that when Jutta was taken away, my dad was changed forever.

At age thirteen, my father had his bar mitzvah in Kassel, Germany. Two uninvited guests showed up—SS men, brown shirts with guns. As my father sang his *parsha*, did his voice crack? I don't know. I imagine him singing beautifully and perfectly in that sweet pitch of a boys voice just before it changes. The SS knew what they were doing. They were trying to intimidate him—intimidate the Jews—break a thirteen-year-old boy's spirit. 1941 Germany, and my father changed into a man.

246

Later, my grandfather secured passage for his family on a ship out of Germany. My grandmother, in the greatest misjudgment of her life, told my grandfather to go to England ahead of them. She couldn't believe that the Nazis would hurt women and children. "Go ahead," she said, "get settled—we'll stay here till we sell our possessions, and then we'll follow." When they tried to follow, it was too late. Their passage had been sold to others. So my grandmother, my dad, and his brother Herman were all ghettoized and then suffered four years in concentration camps, while their father, Isaac, waited for them in London. My dad never spoke much about his father. Did he feel betrayed? Did he feel like his father deserted them? He told me once about their reunion once they had been liberated. He described arriving at the London train station and getting off the train when a man came up to him and said, "Sigi," and he didn't know who he was. My dad, whose memory was always so good, had forgotten his father.

These are some snapshots of my dad's teenage life—a strange life of terror, intimidation and death. He has no photo albums of soccer teams, birthday parties, a high school graduation, or a walk in the park. The imprint of his youth was the knowledge of true evil—first hand, not theoretical. His Mutti, my grandmother, came from a family of 9 children, and all were murdered except for one brother. My grandfather had 5 siblings, and only one brother survived. My dad was cold and starving for probably 1500 days in a row. What kept him alive? When I asked him why he thought he survived, he said it was the eternal optimism of youth. He said it like it was a fact…that all youth are optimistic. Are they? I don't think so. I see plenty of young people who are hardly optimistic. I think optimism was my father's own gift—that and his belief in goodness.

A month before the war ended, my father and his mother and brother were liberated by the Red Cross. He came to this country without any high school education, and proceeded to get a degree in physics from Syracuse University. He married my mother and had four children. When he died in 2000, he had 7 grandchildren, and now he has nine.

My father felt strongly that there were lessons to be learned from the Holocaust. To that end, he and my mother became founders of the United States Holocaust Memorial Museum in Washington D.C. In the opening ceremony at the Rotunda, we all stood as the battalions of U.S. soldiers who fought to liberate the camps marched by us, holding their flags and flags with the camp names. It was one of the only times I ever saw my father cry. He always said that the greatest despair he felt in the camps was the feeling of having been abandoned by the world.

My father never forgot that feeling. Liberated from the death camps, he jumped into life, and never forgot the world that gave him a second chance. He worked harder than any man I've ever seen, not only in his business endeavors, but equally so in his philanthropic ones.

I am sorry that the generation of survivors is dwindling and will soon be gone. They constitute a unique group, a group I am very comfortable with. They provide a doorway into the human condition, into all its richness and poverty. My father's life was an heroic one, because he never succumbed to his suffering. Instead, my father took his suffering and turned it into wisdom. His great hope for humankind rested in understanding and compassion. He never gave up on the world that had SS men at his bar mitzvah, that sent his father away, that imprisoned his family, that starved him, that destroyed eleven uncles and aunts, that murdered his beloved Jutta…never did his suffering or his witness break him. Instead he always reached for the opportunity to make a difference in the world, to be a righteous man and shed light where it can get so very dark. It is my hope that this Institute bearing his name will likewise pursue the lessons to be gleaned from hate so the good in us may prevail.

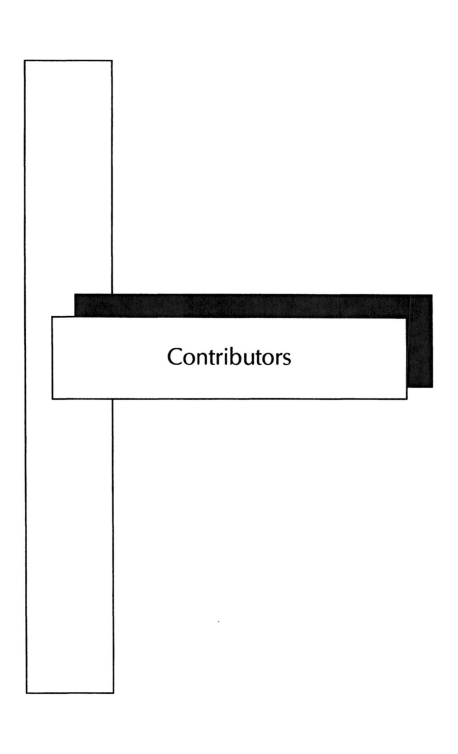

Contributors

Michael Berenbaum is director of the Sigi Ziering Institute: Exploring the Ethical and Religious Implications of the Holocaust and an Adjunct Professor of Theology at the University of Judaism. He is the former President and Chief Executive Officer of the *Survivors of the Shoah Visual History Foundation*. He was the Director of the United States Holocaust Research Institute at the U.S. Holocaust Memorial Museum and the Hymen Goldman Adjunct Professor of Theology at Georgetown University in Washington, D.C. From 1988–93 he served as Project Director of the United States Holocaust Memorial Museum, overseeing its creation. He has written and edited 15 books on the Holocaust, most recently *A Promise to Remember: The Holocaust in the Words and the Voices of Its Survivors.*

Elliot N. Dorff is Rector of the University of Judaism and Distinguished Professor of Philosophy. A Conservative Rabbi, he serves on the Law Committee of the Rabbinical Assembly and is one of the world's leading authorities on Medical Ethics. He is the author of several books including *Matters of Life and Death: A Jewish Approach to Modern Medical Ethics* and *To Do the Right and the Good*, which won the National Jewish Book Award in Jewish Thought for 2003.

Rene Firestone is a survivor of Auschwitz, whose life story was featured in the Academy Award-winning film, *The Last Days.* She has taught at the Simon Wiesenthal Center's Museum of Tolerance Beit Hashoah, and at the Survivors of the Shoah Visual History Foundation.

Eugene Fisher is Director of Catholic-Jewish Relations for the Secretariat for Ecumenical Affairs of the National Conference of Catholic Bishops. He is also Consultor to the Vatican Commision for Religious Relations with the Jews, one of only eight such consultors and the only American. He is the author of sixteen books, including *Visions of the Other: Jewish and Christian Theologians Assess the Dialogue.*

Jonathan Freund is a Masters candidate at the Fingerhut School of Education at the University of Judaism. He assisted significantly in the editing of this manuscript.

Gershon Greenberg teaches in the Department of Philosophy and Religion at American University. His current area of research is the history of Jewish religious thought through the Holocaust. His published studies probe Orthodox responses to the catastrophe from the schools of Hasidism, Musar, Agudat Israel and Mizrachi, as well as Jewish wartime response to Christianity. He has taught the history of modern Jewish religious thought in the Departments of Jewish Thought and Philosophy at Haifa, Tel Aviv and Hebrew University and in the Faculty of Oriental Studies at Oxford University. He has been a Research Fellow at the Finkler Institute for Holocaust Research at Bar-Ilan University.

David H. Jones, the author of *Moral Responsibility in the Holocaust: A Study in the Ethics of Character*, is a Professor at William and Mary in Williamsburg, Virginia [Emeritus].

Robert Melson is a child survivor of the Holocaust and a leading scholar on the Holocaust and genocide. His autobiography, *False Papers: Deception and Survival in the Holocaust* is told in three voices, his own, his father's and his mother's and depicts their life during the Holocaust when his parents pretended to be Polish noblemen living in exile in Prague. He is a Professor of Political Science at Purdue University in Indiana and the author of *Revolution and Genocide: On the Origins of the Armenian Genocide and the Holocaust.*

Didier Pollefeyt teaches Moral Theology and courses on Jewish-Christian relations at Katholieke University Leuven, Belguim, where he serves on the Theology Faculty.

John K. Roth is the Edward J. Sexton Professor of Philosophy and Director, Center for the Study of the Holocaust, Genocide, and Human Rights at Claremont McKenna College. He is recognized as one of the preeminent Christian scholars on the Holocaust and a pioneer in the field of Holocaust Ethics. He is the author of scores of books on the Holocaust and on the American Experience. Among them are: *Holocaust Politics, Approaches to Auschwitz: The Holocaust and Its Legacy* (together with Richard L. Rubenstein); *In Different Voices: Women and the Holocaust* (edited together with Carol Rittner, RSM) and *The Holocaust: Religious and Philosophical Implications* (edited together with Michael Berenbaum) and *Ethics after the Holocaust: Perspectives, Critiques and Responses.* In 1988, Roth was named U.S. Professor of the Year by the Council for Advancement and Support of Education and the Carnegie Foundation for the Advancement of Teaching.

Efraim Zuroff is the director of the Israel office of the Simon Wiesenthal Center and coordinator of Nazi war crimes research (worldwide) for the Center. He is the leading Nazi-hunter of his generation, insisting that the perpetrators of the Holocaust be brought to justice. Zuroff is the author of *The Response of Orthodox Jewry to the Holocaust in the United States.*

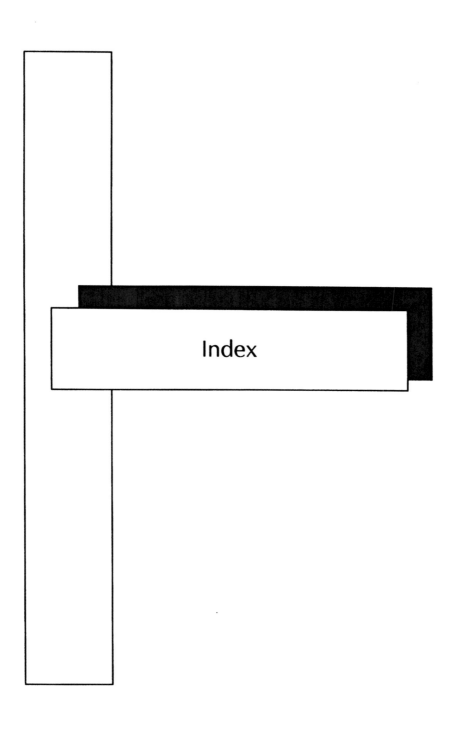

Index

CPSIA information can be obtained at www.ICGtesting.com
Printed in the USA
BVOW03s1924310315

394132BV00001B/16/P